SCANDINAVIAN
GRAPHIC DESIGN

GINGKO PRESS

SCANDINAVIAN GRAPHIC DESIGN

ISBN 978-1-58423-463-0

First Published in the United States of America by Gingko Press
by arrangement with Sandu Publishing Co., Limited

Gingko Press, Inc.
1321 Fifth Street
Berkeley, CA 94710 USA
Tel: (510) 898 1195
Fax: (510) 898 1196
Email: books@gingkopress.com
www.gingkopress.com

Copyright © 2012 by SANDU PUBLISHING

Sponsored by: Design 360° – Concept and Design Magazine
Chief Editor: Wang Shaoqiang
Executive Editor: Yvonne Syan Yi
Chief Designer: Wang Shaoqiang
Book Designers: Leo Cheung, Ginger Lau
Sales Managers:
Niu Guanghui (China), Daniela Huang (International)
Address:
3rd Floor, West Tower,
No.10 Ligang Road, Haizhu District,
510280, Guangzhou, China
Tel: (86)-20-84316758
Fax: (86)-20-84344460
sandu.sales@gmail.com
www.sandu360.com

Cover illustration by Oh Yeah Studio

Printed and bound in China

CONTENTS

FOREWORD

Interview with **HENRIK NYGREN**
Stockholm, Sweden

*"It is functional, doable, long lasting, clean, and simple –
though some of these words are frequently used when you
speak about Swedish graphic design, I think they do define
what it is all about."*

◇◇◇◇◇◇◇◇◇◇

How do you define the style of Swedish graphic design? Where does the minimalistic aesthetic approach come from?

I do not think there is a specific Swedish style of design, but more of a Swedish attitude towards design. It is a general question, but Swedish graphic design is, at its best, functional and has a kind of minimalistic approach. If you brought this kind of design to other parts of the world, like to the United States, it maybe wouldn't work as well. My wife, who is from Canada and has lived in New York for 3 years, and who is also working with graphic design, always says that what we do here in Sweden, based on the working climate and the high demand from clients for good design, is hard to do somewhere else. It is functional, doable, long lasting, clean, and simple – though some of these words are frequently used when you speak about Swedish graphic design, I think they do define what it is all about.

Is Stockholm still inspiring? How do you expect the graphic design and creative industry to continue to develop here?

I think it is a very inspiring city; it has a lot of possibilities. It has a very good climate for design. There are many museums, art galleries and retail stores where you can find very well designed and produced fashion and product design. I believe that the development of Swedish graphic design also has been doing well both domestically and internationally. Going back to the 1940s or 1950s, Swedish design was more about product design or architecture, but later on, graphic design, together with music and fashion design, found its place.

Sweden enjoys a longer design history than the other four Nordic countries, so there is a nickname for Sweden: the Big Brother. What do you think of this? And what role does Swedish design play in Scandinavian design?

Sweden might be called "Big Brother" and I think that is for at least two reasons. One is that Sweden is located in the centre of Scandinavia; we have Finland to the east, Norway, Denmark and Iceland to the west. The other reason I think is that we are the largest country in size and also in population. That is why someone also might call Stockholm the capital of Scandinavia. It is interesting to think about Scandinavia as a region. We share, as all countries, the same ideas when it comes to the attitude towards design in all kind of fields.

Do you think that the design and art world is interacting more broadly and that specific personal, cultural and geographical identities are less important now? How can Scandinavian design survive globalization?

I think Scandinavia, as in all different cultures, is unique in its special way. When it comes to globalization, I think it is important to let what is Swedish be Swedish and what is Chinese be Chinese. The differences are all beautiful, and needed.

*"Visually, the Danish style is probably more
solid, urban and contemporary in its expression,
favoring simplicity over decoration."*

~~~~~~~~~~~~~~~~~~~

How do you define the style of Danish graphic design? Do you think your design output is reminiscent of the Danish heritage?

Danish graphic design, and Danish design in general, is often briefly described with words like minimalistic, clean and cool. But there is more to it than just aesthetics. Danish design is more an idea than a style. There is often a concept behind the visual expression, and functionalism plays a large role – at least in the work we do.

Our work is of course influenced by our surrounding visual culture, and we probably do follow the Danish design heritage. It is not something that we intentionally aim for, but we adhere to the same basic principles of the modernist movement, so the style more or less comes naturally to us. We always aspire to create long-lasting solutions, based on great ideas, well thought out concepts and compelling visual expressions.

Is Copenhagen still inspiring? What are the pros and cons of being a designer here?

Yes, Copenhagen is inspiring. In size, it's in between an urban metropolis and small town, global and local at the same time – and a great city to both live and work in. The city is friendly and open to be explored, and very few places are off limits. There are always a lot of things going on in the cultural scene. There is room for innovation and there is a strong synergy among different creative fields like design, music, architecture, fashion and art in general.

The only con is that living and working in Copenhagen – or anywhere else, for that matter – for a longer period of time, can make you blasé and blind to your surroundings. When you become too familiar with a place, you often miss the underlying qualities and feel less motivated to go searching the city for inspiration. That is why we also like to travel, and continually expose ourselves to new impressions and broaden our horizons.

What role do you think that Danish design plays in the realm of Scandinavian design? How closely does it relate to the other four Nordic countries?

Scandinavian design style is generally characterized by references to the surrounding nature, the dim Nordic light, a faded color palette and a minimalistic approach. But beyond these common sources of inspiration, the individual countries and regions also maintain their own typical styles.

Danish design style is less rooted in local tradition and folklore than our neighboring countries. Denmark is a smaller country, has less spectacular nature and is generally more oriented towards the rest of Europe – and that reflects in the visual culture. While the design styles of the other Nordic regions often make use of illustration, patterns and ornaments relating to their national heritage of arts and crafts, Danish design is more influenced by international tendencies and ideas of modernism and functionalism. Visually, the Danish style is probably more solid, urban and contemporary in its expression, favoring simplicity over decoration.

Do you think that the design and art world is interacting more broadly and that specific personal, cultural and geographical identities are less important now? How can Scandinavian design survive globalization?

No, we don't believe that globalization will make local identities less important. On the contrary, as the world becomes more and more globalized, complex and blurred, the need for unity, togetherness and community will rise. Globalization sparks localization – and national and geographical visual culture will continue to develop as a counter-reaction. The global context will strengthen the local expression.

The style of Scandinavian design will naturally change over time, but it will continue to be Scandinavian design, simply because it is designed in Scandinavia. Specific trends and styles can be copied and adapted, but the unique Scandinavian approach and way of thinking cannot.

"We are all trying to make things work better; that is what design is about, evolving in every aspect and detail, and when a culture embraces this it actually works."

~~~~~~

What do you think defines Norwegian graphic design? Do you think it relies more on form or concept? How have design approaches evolved over the years?

I think there are a lot of different styles going on in Norwegian design. A lot of designers have studied abroad and took the influences they encountered home with them. Also everyone follows everything that is happening around them. At Bleed we have always measured ourselves against the world and not what is going on locally.

That said, there are lifestyle influences and states of mind that make the design approach unique. Norwegians (like most Scandinavians) are practical people, we don't like a big fuss or complicating a message. There is a matter of fact approach in how we communicate with not too much politeness or unnecessary decoration. I think this makes Norwegian and Scandinavian design cleaner and to the point. In these cases the form becomes the message and concept. We see the same in industrial design and architecture.

What role do you think Norwegian design plays in the realm of Scandinavian design? How closely does Norwegian design relate to design in the other four Nordic countries?

Norway is one of the latest players from Scandinavia. Denmark, Finland and Sweden have been using design way more intentionally for far longer than us. This makes us the challenger that is a bit less afraid of making mistakes. It feels like there are a greater variety of things coming out of Norway right now.

Norway is small but the number of people working in creative industries is huge. How do you expect Norwegian design to develop in the future?

I am not sure that this statement is true?

I think there is a good growing culture for understanding the importance of design in all areas of society. The shared knowledge of design pushes designers to deliver better and more thought out concepts. I think this is a global phenomenon though. We are all trying to make things work better; that is what design is about, evolving in every aspect and detail, and when a culture embraces this it actually works.

Could you share some of your experiences working and living in Oslo? Is it still inspiring? What are the pros and cons of being a designer in Oslo?

Working and living in Oslo is not too bad. Oslo is large enough that things happen but small enough that is feels intimate. Even for its small size, with only about 500,000 living in the central area, Oslo has more concerts a year than Stockholm and Copenhagen combined. Oslo is also close to nature, with both the forest and sea close by. In summer you can take a boat out to the surrounding islands and go swimming, in winter you can ski. Oslo is also a great hub for traveling. It is easy and relatively cheap to fly to most destinations directly from OSL airport.

We have an international culture at Bleed with people from France, Switzerland, Russia, Austria and Sweden working in the office. We also most times have interns from different parts of the world. They all feel Oslo has a calmness to it that they like. You can live in the city with not too much stress.

I think a definitive pro for me as a designer in Norway is the difference between seasons. I love the contrast between the dark cold of winter and the sunny blue skies, green grass, and blue water of summer. Parts of winter have only very few hours of light, perfect for concentrating on work. Summer has only a few dark hours, so it's perfect for getting new energy. A con of course is that the city's a bit smaller and less diverse in the types of residents and design challenges - but we can always go abroad.

Interview with **MAGNUS HELGESEN**
GRANDPEOPLE
Bergen, Norway

"To us, design matters because we want things to work properly, last for a long time and not destroy the world. We also find meaning in harmonious proportions, good stories and challenging messages."

How do you define the style of Norwegian graphic design? Do you think it relies more on form than concept? Do design approaches change in any way during these years?

We don't think there is such a thing as Norwegian graphic design. Historically the styles and techniques in the Norwegian design field have changed according to international trends, and Norway never got around to developing a significant, national style. Lacking a defined tradition can also be seen as a blessing. There's a liberal attitude where "everything goes", which we think is inspiring and good. But since it is hard to define what exactly a Norwegian style of graphic design is, we feel it would be wrong to say it relates more to form or more to concept. In Norway we get all kinds. That being said, one can perhaps argue that during the last 10 years, there has been a tendency within the trade toaward projects where form has played a central role. In several cases the conceptual foundation might have been to establish a story, to create the right sensation, and then the graphic design became the conveyor of this story through form.

What role do you think that Norwegian design plays in the realm of Scandinavian design? How closely does it relate to the other four Nordic countries?

To tell you the truth, I don't think the other Scandinavian countries pay much attention to what happens in Norway. Denmark, Sweden and Finland all have a strong design heritage, have a larger population and are big cultural and academic producers, while Norway is mostly seen as the role of the uneducated little brother. Iceland is also a sort of cultural outsider amongst the Nordic countries, which has resulted in several artistic surprises over the years. So I think this outsider role can be a blessing and a curse.

Norway is small but many people work in creative industries, and there are a lot of creative activities. How do you expect Norwegian design to develop?

Hopefully we'll see more experimentation and creative exploration. There are so many other designers in the world who are experts in the science of type design and information design. I think we ought to see our lack of tradition as a possibility to explore.

Though Norway doesn't enjoy a very long history of design, its current development is quite impressive. Do you think design is highly regarded in Norway? What do you think design means to Norwegians?

I think a large part of the Norwegian population still considers the term "design" as a fancy wrapping you apply to a product or brand at the end of the production line, and it's absolutely a matter of taste and class. Many Norwegian businesses, which have prospered for years without a proper design strategy, didn't really see how design could improve efficiency and increase project success. I think it's correct to say that this mentality is changing.

To us design matters because we want things to work properly, last for a long time and not destroy the world. We also find meaning in harmonious proportions, good stories and challenging messages.

Is Bergen still inspiring? What are the pros and cons of being a designer here?

It's inspiring in the sense that the creative environment is rather big in comparison to the size of the town. Everybody knows each other, and collaborations are quite common. Still, Bergen is a small and isolated town.

Interview with **JOHANNES EKHOLM**
TSTO
Helsinki, Finland

"Design has to overcome the notion of being just a question of style. Design is a process of understanding and making things understandable."

• • • • • • • •

<u>What are three words you think describe the Finnish graphic design experience - and why?</u>
Rational. Evolving. Experimental.

I think the roots of Finnish design are easily visible. Modernism had a great impact; for a long time design depended on functionality. Recently there's been a shift towards a more playful and emotional approach. The post-war seriousness is giving way to a more experimental attitude.

<u>Design Forum Finland started promoting design 130 years ago - before Finland even became a country, so there's a long history of design here. Do you think things here will ever be over-designed? You've said that since Finland is so small, the city of Helsinki is everything to you - is it still inspiring as a design center?</u>
Finland's always been on the periphery of Europe, so phenomena have long had an impact later here compared to other European countries. Geography plays a role, though the internet has of course narrowed the gap a little bit. History plays a role; compared to Sweden we've been slow to embrace a globalized attitude. But nevertheless, something is rapidly changing. Helsinki being chosen to be World Design Capital 2012 is a great sign. The tagline "Embedding Design in Life" is a good challenge: design should not be something just on the surface; it should be integrated in life, it should make life easier, it should increase happiness. If it's done right, I don't think anything can be over-designed.

<u>We can always find Illustration frequently applied in Finnish graphic design. And some of the designers are also illustrators as well. So where does this illustrated aesthetic approach come from?</u>
If you look back, Finland has a great history in the visual arts. The Finnish national identity was basically built around poetry and painting. The golden era of visual arts in Finland took place during the oppression in 1880-1910, when Finland was still under governmental policy of the Russian Empire. Painters such as Axeli Gallen-Kallela and Albert Edelfelt laid the foundation for Finnish nationalism and thus contributed to independence in 1918. In contemporary illustration you can still see influences from Gallen-Kallela, or for example the symbolist Hugo Simberg. In the 1940s and 1950s came Tove Jansson's Moomin figures and Jansson's style still inspires generation after generation. Mid-century advertising followed European and North American illustration trends, and designers such as Erik Bruun, Ingrid Bade and Osmo K. Oksanen had a great impact on later designers and illustrators. Many internationally recognized illustrators today continue in these paths, either intentionally or unconsciously.

<u>How closely does Finnish design relate to that of the other four Nordic countries? Do you think they have any similar elements of style? Are there many forms of creative exchange between the countries?</u>
There are definitely a lot of similarities in style and ways of thinking. The influence of modernism is very clear in all of the Nordic countries. For Swedes it's relatively easy to come and work in Finland, and for Finns who learn the mandatory Swedish in school it's even easier to move to Sweden. And Swedish is very close to the other Nordic languages, Norwegian and Danish.

<u>Do you think that the design and art world is interacting more broadly and that specific personal, cultural and geographical identities are less important now? How can Scandinavian design survive globalization?</u>
I don't see globalization as a cultural threat. I think it's great we have the internet! I love the fast pace of visual trends! But on a bigger scale I think design is subject to global political and economic changes. Europe will depend more and more on Asia. And what happens in Europe in the next ten years will define what chances Finland and the rest of the Scandinavian countries have in the global market. Will the economic and monetary union in Europe fall apart? Will the cultural climate in Europe change further towards a hostile nationalism, close borders, racism and growing class differences? Or will the EU overcome its economic difficulties and even form a super-national federation? Finland's future is dependent on a high level of expertise in technology, economy and the arts. Maybe a certain humanism founded in the social democratic tradition gives the Scandinavian countries good standing to function as a diplomatic link in international affairs. I think design has to overcome the notion of being just a question of style. Design is a process of understanding and making things understandable. A Scandinavian design approach is simply a means to this end.

GRANDPEOPLE
Norway

Since the start in 2005, Grandpeople have worked with a range of clients from every part of the world. Grandpeople provide different and distinctive solutions in graphic design, art direction, photography and illustration.

2010

The Alexandria Quartet "Light Drawings"

Identity and album artwork for Norwegian pop/rock ensemble.

-

Client
The Alexandria Quartet

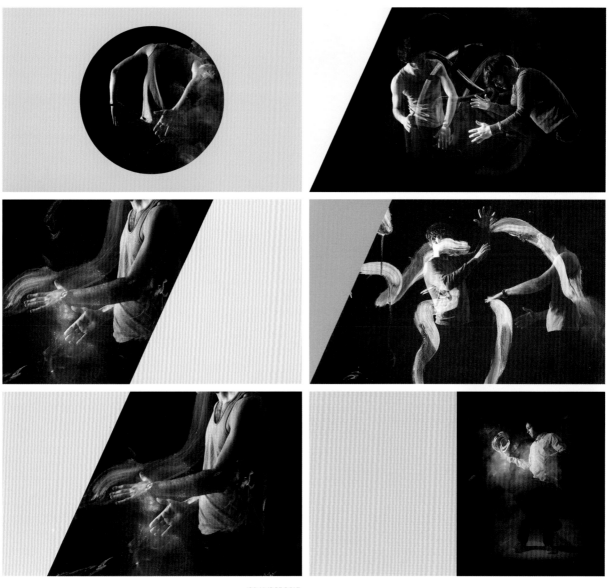

2010

The New Wine - Waves

"Waves" is the debut album of The New Wine, a band described as some four guys creating guitar and synth based pop with light riffs, aesthetic bass and steady beats.
-
Client
The New Wine

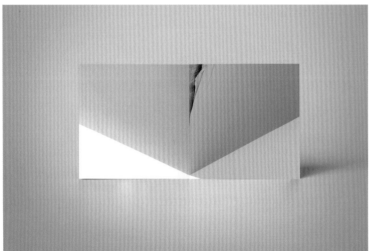

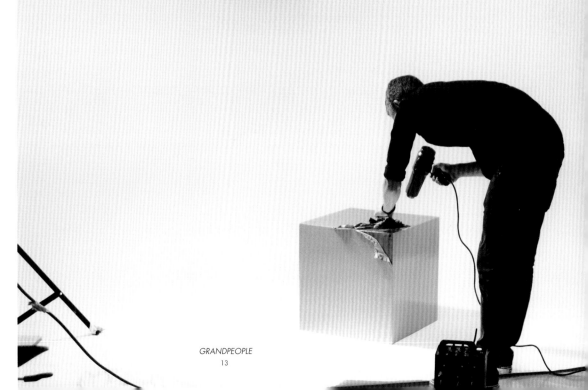

2009
Ekko 2009

Visual profile for electronic music and art festival, created with transparent thermoplastic and photography. The visual concept is based on the idea of echos as reflections of sound. When designing the logo, we concentrated on shapes that somehow would translate into 3-dimensional objects. We then cut the logo from plexi glass, and reused the pieces in separate photographic compositions for decorative purposes.

-
Client
Ekko Festival

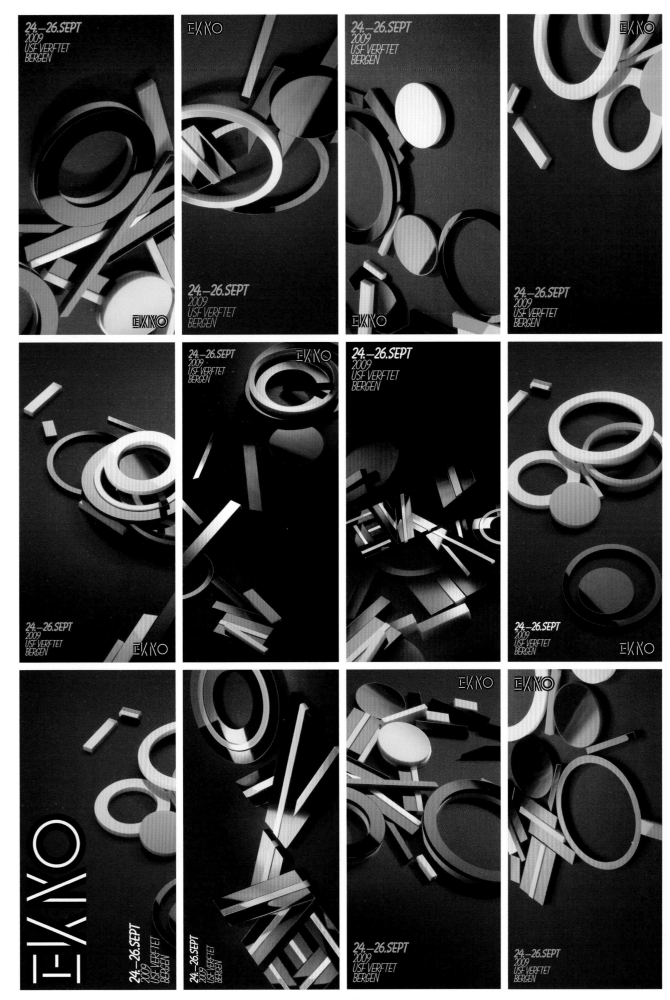

2010

Idrettsårbok 2010

There's a direct link between sports
and statistics, which is called
math. The idea of measuring and
comparing results is what makes
sports so entertaining, and we
wanted to apply this idea when
designing this annual report for
Bergen City's Department of Sports
and Culture.
-
Client
Municipality of Bergen City

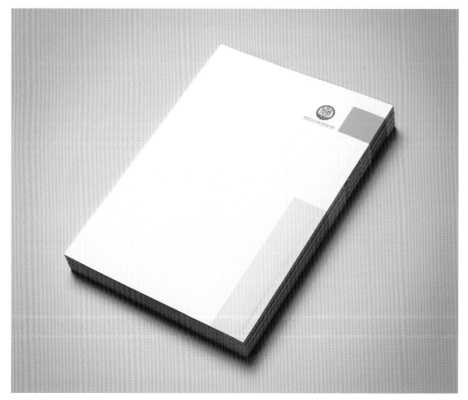

2009

Biennial Conference

The City of Bergen wanted to start up a biennial for visual arts, and asked Bergen Kunsthall to host the international art symposium "Bergen Biennial Conference". The identity is based around questions and uncertainty. Should there, or should there not be a biennial in Bergen? Nobody knows exactly where the biennial as a phenomenon is heading, and this ambiguity is reflected in the juxtaposition of the illustrative elements and the slogan "to biennial or not to biennial".

–
Client
Bergen Kunsthall

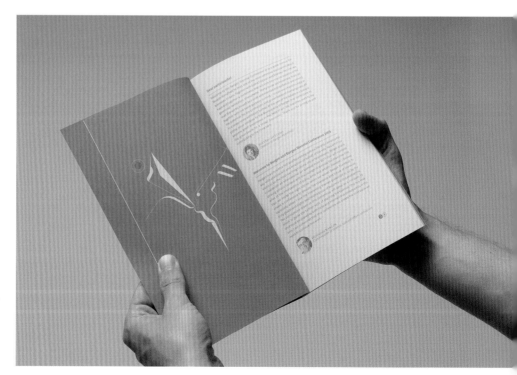

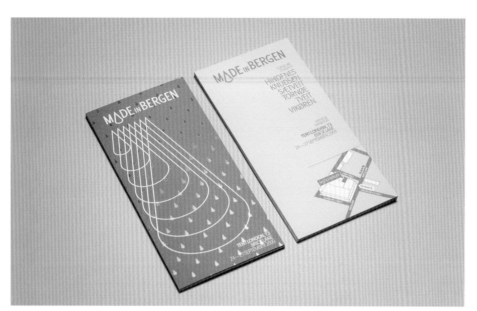

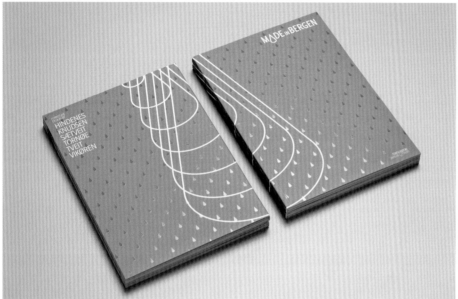

2009
Made in Bergen

In the exhibition project "Made in Bergen", six furniture and interior designers joined forces to demonstrate what Bergen has to offer as a growing design centre. The visual concept represents Bergen quite literally by means of two stereotypical features of the city: Seven overlapping shapes can be viewed as raindrops, or as seven mountains – reduced and simplified to cone shapes.

Client
Tveit & Tornøe, Knudsen & Hindenes, Geir Sætveit, Dave Vikøren

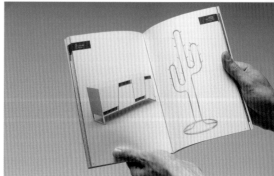

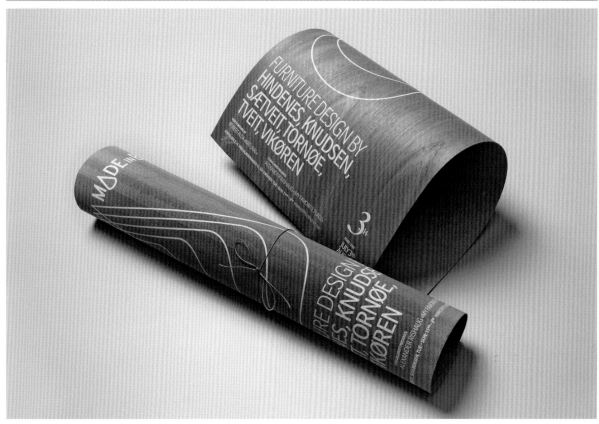

MVM
Norway

〜〜〜

MVM, or Magnus Voll Mathiassen (*1979), works as an independent art director, graphic designer and illustrator. He co-founded the Norwegian design studio Grandpeople in 2005. The studio received international acclaim during his years. He left the studio in 2009 and set up his own practice MVM.
He has created his very own visual language that gains a broader audience every day. His work is mainly for print, but uses a growing roster of talents from various creative fields to explore all types of media. Mathiassen lives and works in Drammen, Norway.

2010

The Perennial Medium

The Perennial Medium is a record with experimental contemporary music.
It is somewhat an album that mocks its musical genre by being extremely pretentious. The cover design reflects some sort of bygone modernistic aesthetics, referring to old (outdated) experimental music.
-
Client
Safe As Milk
Photography
Magne Sandnes

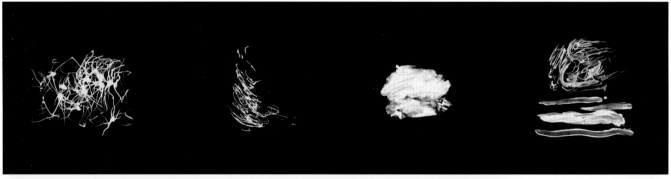

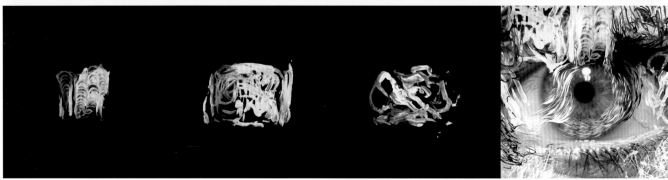

2008

Juvelen "1"

Translated, "Juvelen" means "The Jewel". Juvelen is a pop artist, heavily influenced by Prince. His name and just naming the debut album "1" tells a whole lot about his future path. He makes something for the ladies and something for the rest of us with his electronic touch and pop sensibility.

-

<u>Client</u>
Hybris Records
<u>Ilustration</u>
Grandpeople

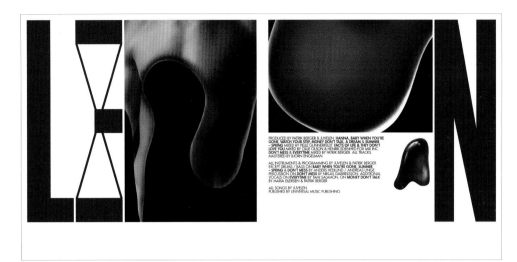

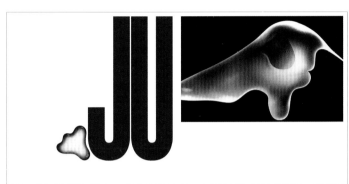

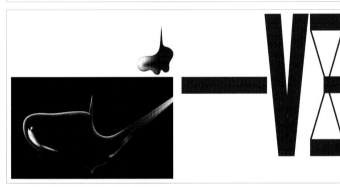

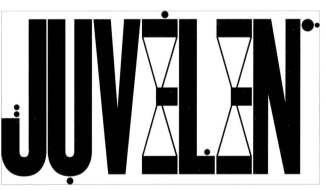

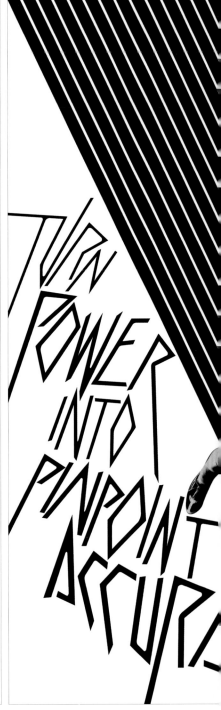

2009

<u>Nike Football Europe – Visual Research</u>

The posters made for Nike Europe were created
to work as a reference source for the Nike team
for further development of the Nike Football
brand. Only used as in-house research material.
-
<u>Client</u>
Nike Europe

2010

<u>Grafik Magazine — Music Special</u>

The May issue of Grafik Magazine was a Music Special with the future of the music industry as its main subject.

-

<u>Client</u>
Grafik Magazine

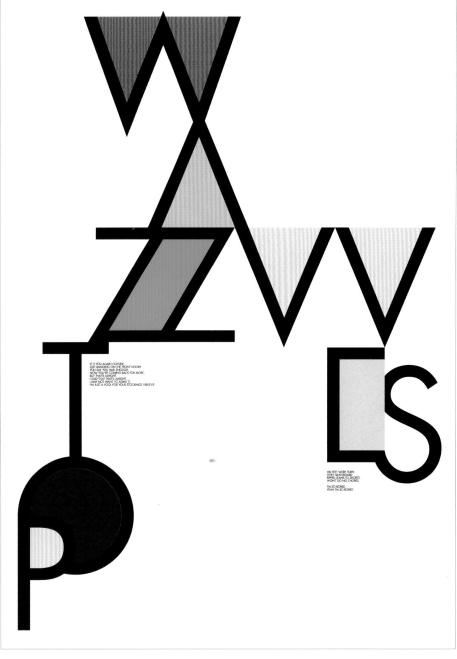

2011

Fra Lippo Lippi CD Compilation

Fra Lippo Lippi is a Norwegian pop trio
from the 1980s. This collector's album
compilation was limited to 500 copies
made specifically for the die-hard fans.

Client
Rune Grammofon

1 A Little Rain Must Fall
2 Mother's Little Soldier
3 Under The Same Sun
4 You Bring Me Joy
5 Love Is A Lonely Harbour
6 Count On Me
7 ABC
8 Childhood Days
9 Into The Blue

THE COLOUR ALBUM

ALBUM
First released in 1989

MUSIC BY SØRENSEN: 3, 4, 6, 7, 8
MUSIC BY KRISTOFFERSEN: 1, 2, 5, 9
ALL LYRICS BY KRISTOFFERSEN

FRA LIPPO LIPPI
RUNE KRISTOFFERSEN: BASS
PER ØYSTEN SØRENSEN: VOCALS, GRAND PIANO AND KEYBOARDS

ADDITIONAL MUSICIANS
MATS ALSBERG, TORE ELGARØY, LASSE HAFREAGER, PER HILLESTAD, BENDIK HOFSETH, HENRIK JANSON, BJØRN JŒ
MARIT KLOVNING, PER LINDVALL, BERIT LOHNE, NILS PETTER MOLVÆR, STIG-OVE OSE, MAGNUS PERSSON, KNUT RII
MAURO SCOCCO, ATLE SPONBERG, CARL ANDERS SPONBERG AND ARILD STAV

PRODUCED BY JOHAN EKELUND, RUNE KRISTOFFERSEN AND PER ØYSTEN SØRENSEN
RECORDED BY JOHAN EKELUND AT RAINBOW STUDIOS, OSLO
ADDITIONAL RECORDINGS BY JAN ERIK KONGSHAUG, ESPEN DAHL AND BERNARD LOHR
MIXED BY BERNARD LOHR AND JOHAN EKELUND AT POLAR STUDIOS, STOCKHOLM
5, 6 AND 9 MIXED AT BEL STUDIOS, OSLO

1 Come Summer
2 Shouldn't Have To Be Like That
3 Even Tall Trees Bend
4 Just Like Me
5 Crash Of Light
6 The Distance Between Us
7 Regrets
8 Leaving
9 Coming Home

SONGS

ALBUM
First released in 1985

MUSIC BY KRISTOFFERSEN, KVALNES, SJØBERG AND SØRENSEN: 1, 6 AND 8
MUSIC BY KRISTOFFERSEN: 2 AND 4
MUSIC BY KRISTOFFERSEN AND KVALNES: 5
MUSIC BY KRISTOFFERSEN, SJØBERG AND SØRENSEN: 3
MUSIC BY KVALNES: 7
ALL LYRICS BY KRISTOFFERSEN EXCEPT 7 BY KVALNES

FRA LIPPO LIPPI
RUNE KRISTOFFERSEN: BASS, KEYBOARDS
ØIVIND KVALNES: KEYBOARDS
MORTEN SJØBERG: DRUMS AND PROGRAMMING
PER ØYSTEN SØRENSEN: VOCALS AND KEYBOARDS

ADDITIONAL MUSICIAN
ERIK HAUSLER: SAX ON 5 AND 7

PRODUCED BY KAJ ERIXON
DIGITALLY RECORDED AT POLAR STUDIOS, STOCKHOLM JAN-FEB 1985
2005 REMASTERING BY MORTEN LUND AT MASTERHUSET, OSLO

1 Angel
2 Freedom
3 Don't Take Away That Light
4 Beauty And Madness
5 Home
6 Light And Shade
7 Some People
8 Crazy Wisdom
9 Stardust Motel
10 Indifference

LIGHT AND SHADE

ALBUM
First released in 1987

MUSIC BY SØRENSEN: 1, 3, 4, 5, 6 AND 7
MUSIC BY KRISTOFFERSEN: 8 AND 10
MUSIC BY KRISTOFFERSEN AND SØRENSEN: 2 AND 9
ALL LYRICS BY KRISTOFFERSEN

FRA LIPPO LIPPI
RUNE KRISTOFFERSEN: BASS
PER ØYSTEIN SØRENSEN: VOCALS AND GRAND PIANO

ADDITIONAL MUSICIANS
WALTER BECKER, ROBBIE BUCHANON, LEROY CLOUDEN, PAULINHO DA COSTA, JIMMY HASLIP, MARK ISHAM, JAMES JOHNSON,
ABE LABORIAL, MARK MORGAN, DEAN PARKS, CLAUDE PEPPER, JEFF PORCARO, TOM SCOTT, CARLOS VEGA AND TIM WESTON

PRODUCED BY WALTER BECKER
ENGINEERED AND MIXED BY ROGER NICHOLS, ASSISTED BY RUSSELL BRACHER
MASTERED BY BOB LUDWIG AT MASTERDISK

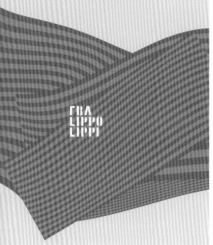

1 Thief In Paradise
2 Living In A Crazy World
3 Naive
4 Not Invited
5 Heart Of The Matter
6 Stitches And Burns
7 One World
8 Wonderful Day
9 Dreams

DREAMS

ALBUM
First released in 1992

MUSIC BY SØRENSEN : 1, 4, 5, 6, 8 AND 9
MUSIC BY KRISTOFFERSEN : 2, 3 AND 7
ALL LYRICS BY KRISTOFFERSEN

FRA LIPPO LIPPI
RUNE KRISTOFFERSEN : BASS AND KEYBOARDS
PER ØYSTEIN SØRENSEN : VOCALS AND KEYBOARDS

ADDITIONAL MUSICIANS
OTTAR NESJE : DRUMS
TOM PETTERSEN : GUITARS

PRODUCED BY FRA LIPPO LIPPI
RECORDED BY RUNE KRISTOFFERSEN AT EASTER SOUND STUDIO
MIXED BY KAJ ERIXON AT ROB STUDIO

LIGHT AND SHADE

Liner notes by Rune Kristoffersen, 2011
Design by MVM

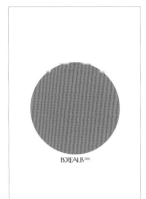

27

34

35

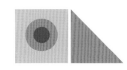

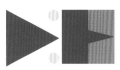

61

66

67

2010

Borealis Festival 2010

Borealis is a new festival for contemporary music and has become one of the most interesting festivals of its kind in Scandinavia. The festival line-up is very diverse. Everything from rusty punk and disco to classical music. Every year is thematically different. Logo and typeface is strongly influenced by Norwegian Dragon style and old architecture, as well as the mix of serif and sans serif grotesques to emphasize the meeting of the extreme variations in the musical line-ups.

Client
Borealis Festival

BOREANA

9-13

MARS

BOREALIS 2010

BERGEN FESTIVAL FOR CONTEMPORARY MUSIC
WWW.BOREALISFESTIVAL.NO

BERGEN

Sweden

Bergen is a Stockholm-based graphic design studio
established in 2005. The studio was founded by Hanne
Lindberg, after graphic design studies at Beckmans
College of Design in Stockholm, and a period of working
at Practise (James Goggin) in London. Apart from being
a designer, Hanne is also a musician and DJ, and a
member of the editorial staff at *Ful* magazine.
Bergen works on a diverse range of commissions across
various scales, budgets and media. Experimenting is an
important part of Bergen's practice and the work often
includes paper, folding, formats, making typefaces,
painting, drawing and such.

STOLTA LITAUER VÄGRADE TYSTAS

2007-2011

Ful – Art magazine

Ful is a queer feminist art publication.
Hanne is also an editor of *Ful*. The
magazine publishes art. The cover
of *Ful* is always made together with
illustrator Alexandra Falagara. *Ful* also
throws parties now and then, of which
the party poster has hand drawn typo
by Bergen.
-
Client
Ful
Design
Hanne Lindberg
Illustration
Alexandra Falagara, Anna Giertz etc
Photography
Elisabeth Ohlson Wallin, Sophie Mörner etc

2010

Familjen – Mänskligheten

Familjen is a Swedish electronic
artist. He creates music by mixing
analogue and digital sounds.
Cutting up the photographs made
Familjen look strange and unhuman,
like a troll almost.
-
Client
Adrian Recordings / Hybris
Design & Collage
Hanne Lindberg
Photography
Erik Wåhlström

2010

Stad #3 Confluence Belgrade

Stad is an architecture magazine made by a group of Swedish artists. Each number is made by different designers. This number is edited by two Serbian artists and printed in Belgrade. The magazine contains documentation from "wanderlust" – walking in the city as a way to get to know an unknown place. The format and folding is like a map and is also a bit ungainly as maps usually are.

-

<u>Client</u>
Stad – Architecture magazine
<u>Design</u>
Hanne Lindberg

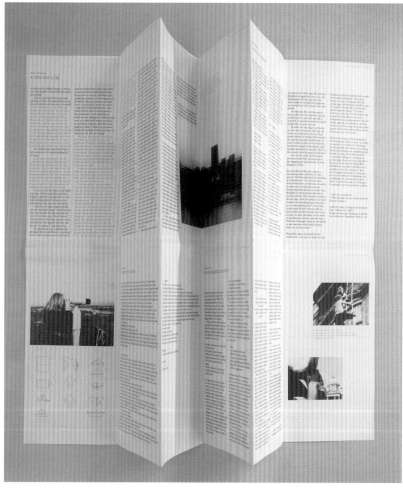

2006
[Right] Påsen

Påsen means "bag" in Swedish. It is a self-initiated project made by Bergen and some friends. Writers and artists were invited to contribute and the fanzine was produced with a photocopier in A4 and A3 format. The edges were cut and the sheets were folded and collected into a small brown paper bag. Another issue is hopefully coming up soon.

–
Client
Self-initiated
Design
Hanne Lindberg
Photography
Johan Avedal etc

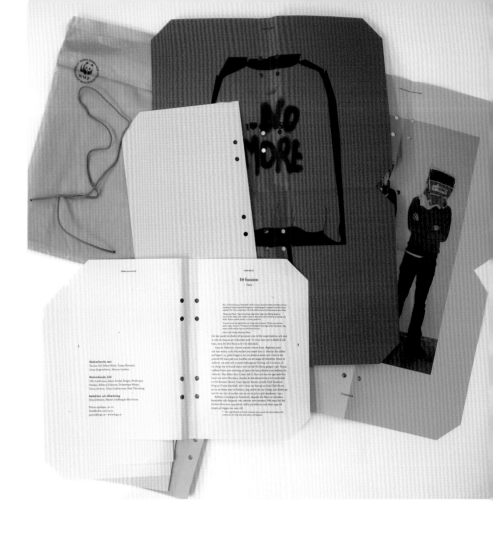

2006
[Left] Bookmark

The bookmark was commissioned by Norrköping Public Library. The bookmarks were handed out to young readers encouraging them to write their own novels.
–
Client
Norrköping Public Library
Design
Hanne Lindberg

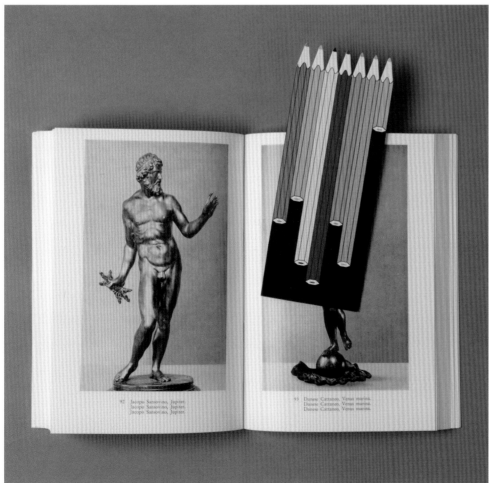

2009

Stuck Inside of Mobile

Invite design for an exhibition with furniture
by designer Mattias Karlsson. The furniture
is also designed as animal characters.

■
Client
Royal College of Art, Stockholm
Design & Illustration
Hanne Lindberg

˘STUCK˘
INSIDE OF
MOBILE
~

MATTIAS KARLSSON
Examensutställning · Kungl. Konsthögskolan
Galleri Mejan · Excersisplan 3 Skeppsholmen
21 februari – 4 mars 2009 · kl 12–18
Vernissage 21 februari · kl 15–18

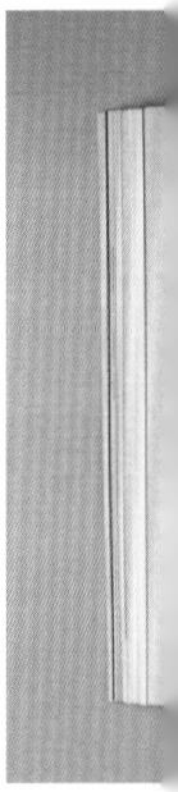

2009

[Above] <u>Vestoj #1</u>

The first issue of Vestoj, a theoretical fashion magazine. The magazine has a different format and design for each issue. This one is themed as "Material Memories" (or the past present in the future) and deals with topics such as nostalgia and historicism in fashion and personal memories of much loved pieces of clothing.

<u>Client</u>
Vestoj ®C Fashion Magazine
<u>Design</u>
Hanne Lindberg, Johanna Jonsson
<u>Illustration</u>
Jenny Mörtsell, Hanna Wieslander, etc
<u>Photography</u>
Martina Hoogland, Katerina Jebb, etc

2007

[Right] <u>Contagion</u>

Invite for "Contagion", a show with several performing artists exploring the act of miming.

<u>Client</u>
Weld Art Gallery, Stockholm
<u>Design & Illustration</u>
Hanne Lindberg

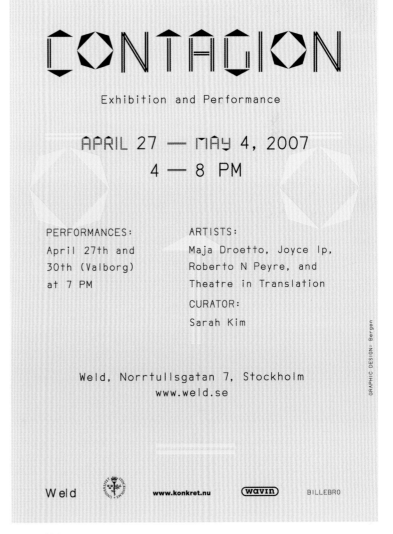

CONTAGION

Exhibition and Performance

APRIL 27 — MAY 4, 2007
4 — 8 PM

PERFORMANCES:
April 27th and
30th (Valborg)
at 7 PM

ARTISTS:
Maja Droetto, Joyce Ip,
Roberto N Peyre, and
Theatre in Translation

CURATOR:
Sarah Kim

Weld, Norrtullsgatan 7, Stockholm
www.weld.se

GRAPHIC DESIGN: Bergen

Weld   www.konkret.nu   wavin   BILLEBRO

TSTO
Finland

●●●●●●●●●●

Tsto is a creative consultancy founded by six designers. They are graphic design professionals specializing in coming up with ideas and visualizing them. Their approach is thorough and hands-on. They tackle an assignment by first taking it apart to its bare essentials, and then building it in a new way that best serves the client. This design philosophy let them go deeper than the surface, to the essence of each case. They also work with other proven professionals in whatever medium the work requires. Instead of competing with other creatives or agencies, they see themselves as possible collaborators for best serving every case.
Tsto was founded by Johannes Ekholm, Jonatan Eriksson, Inka Järvinen, Matti Kunttu, Jaakko Pietiläinen and Antti Uotila.

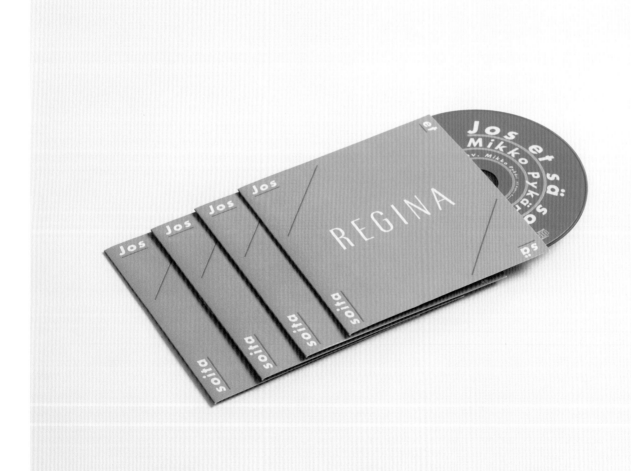

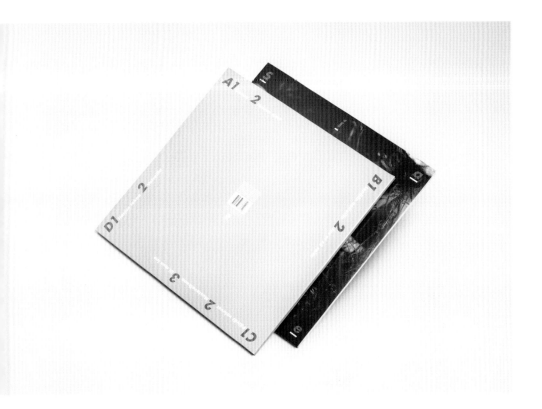

2011

Regina - Soita Mulle

Regina is a three-piece band consisting of husband and wife duo Mikko and Iisa, and a third wheel also going by the name Mikko. "Soita Mulle" is their fourth album and is heavily influenced by the youth and indie music of the 1990s. A new logo and sleeves were created for the singles and the album.
-
Client
Regina / Universal Music Finland
Photography
Megan McIsaacs

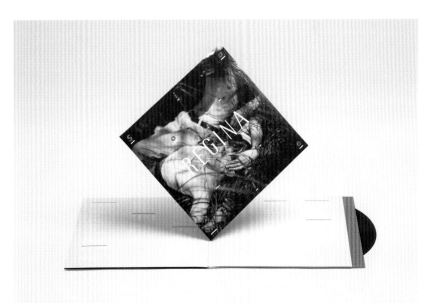

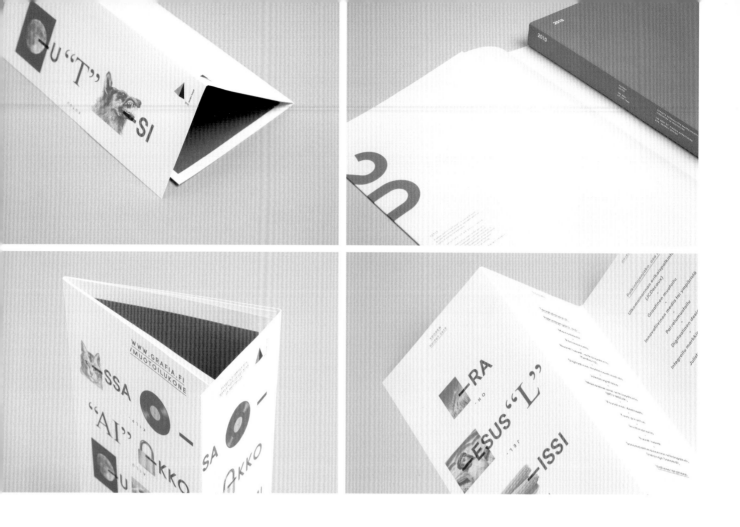

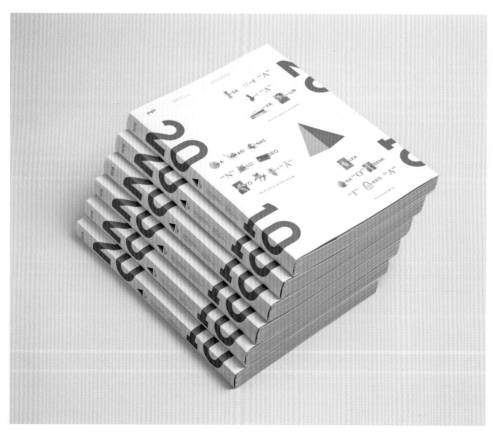

2011

<u>Vuoden Huiput - Best of the Year 2010</u>

With Vuoden Huiput (The Best of the Year in Finnish Advertising and Design) we wanted to experiment with the relatively dubious and unpredictable nature of crowd sourcing and the visual language of anonymous internet users. Together with a programmer we created an application that transformed any written word or sentence into a rebus, an allusion device that uses pictures to represent words or parts of words. In English, a rebus often uses homonyms, as seen in the classic IBM logo consisting of a picture of an eye, a picture of a bee and the letter M. However, homonyms are rare in Finnish language; therefore the rebus is constructed from a list of some 5000 words with the most used syllables and matched with an image search result from Google. The combinations of images and letters may seem just a visual gimmick at first glance, but they challenge the audience to look beneath the mere surface.

-

<u>Client</u>
Grafia
<u>Web Application</u>
Juhani Pelli

Restaurant Gaijin

Located in an excellent spot in the heart of Helsinki, the restaurant opened its doors in April of 2011. Gaijin focuses on North Asian cuisine, combining the traditional with the contemporary. Tsto stepped in to create the visual identity for this fantastic new restaurant.

-

<u>Client</u>
Restaurant Gaijin
<u>Photography</u>
Tuukka Koski

2011

A SONG AND A REASON

For the new Kemopetrol album we created a special typeface as a counterpart to Ea Vasko's beautifully abstract photographs. Central to her photographs is the question of how many or how few recognizable elements our brain needs in order to form a complete visual perception. We found the approach similar to that of Russian Constructivism as well as the Bauhaus movement. The font is a contemporary interpretation of these ideas, stripped down to a minimum of elements, consisting of mainly circles and lines, yet hitting a slightly unorthodox tone.

-

Client
Kemopetrol / Warner Music
Photography
Ea Vasko

2011

El Camino

El Camino is the audio design
studio of Marko Nyberg, a visual
artist and producer. We based
El Camino's identity around an
embossing stamp and a modular
typeface created for the project.

<u>Client</u>
El Camino

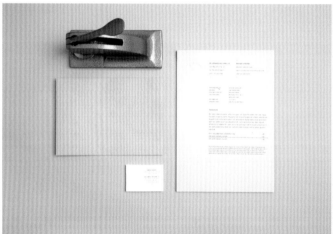

El Camino /
Husky Rescue
typeface

Opium frequently leads to bad palpitations, hazy judgement, and causes weak sex drive... 9 8 7 6 5 4 3 2 1 0 !

2011

Flow Festival

The identity for Flow Festival builds on the idea of the festival crowd as an urban tribe, united by a metaphorical mantra of visual wordplay. The bespoke Flow-typeface is influenced by the contemporary central European trend of postmodern craftsmanship. We see the font as smart, easy to approach and possessing a sense of humor. Together with the illustrations by Santtu Mustonen, the repetition of letters and images creates the core visual language and imagery for the project.
-
<u>Client</u>
Flow Festival
<u>Illustration</u>
Santtu Mustonen
<u>Website</u>
Byroo

ABCDEFGHIJKLMNOPQRSTUVW
abcdefghijklmnopqrstuvwx
23456789!"#$%&'()*+,-.:;<
]^_`{|}~¡¢£¥|§¨©ª«®°±²³´
¿ÀÁÂÃÄÅÆÈÉÊËÌÍÎÏ-ÑÒÓÔÕÖ×
ÞßàáâãäåæèéêëìíîïÐñòóôõ
üýÞÿı
•…‰‹›
ЂЌЎЏ
ЧШЩЪ
уфхц

ÄÖ
01
[\
½ ⅓
ÜÝ
ú û

OSCAR PASTARUS
Sweden

◇◇◇◇◇◇◇◇◇◇◇◇

Oscar Pastarus, born in Stockholm, Sweden in 1986, is a graphic designer and illustrator who previously spent time working in Rome, Italy. Currently he's freelancing from Stockholm. He works in graphic design, typography, illustration and anything in-between.

2010
Lil Wayne

Portrait of Lil Wayne.
-
Client
Self-initiated

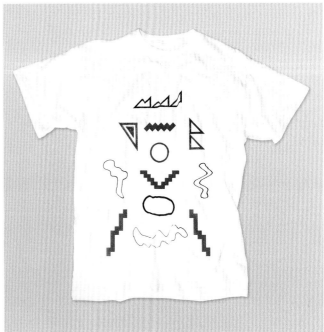

[Top to bottom]

2011
<u>Flying A</u>

T-shirt designs for Flying A's S/S and A/W 2011 collections.

<u>T-Shirt Store</u>

One of several designs Pastarus made for the Swedish based t-shirt brand "T-Shirt Store." About the design: The original Greek sculpture iconography has been described as pale and boring by art historians. This design shows how you can make things more fun – just bring out the spray can!

-
<u>Client</u>
T-Shirt Store and Flying A

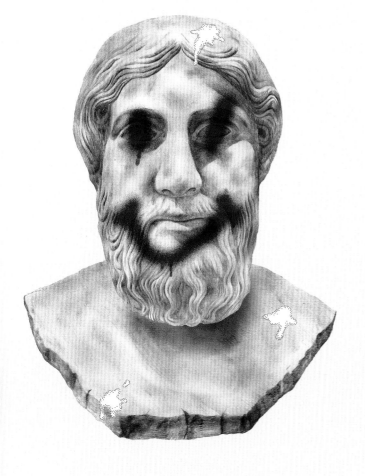

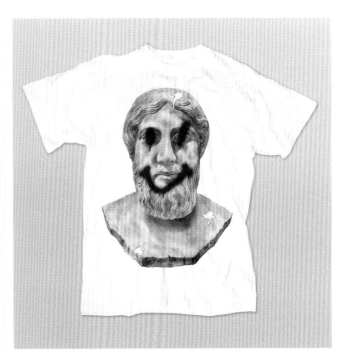

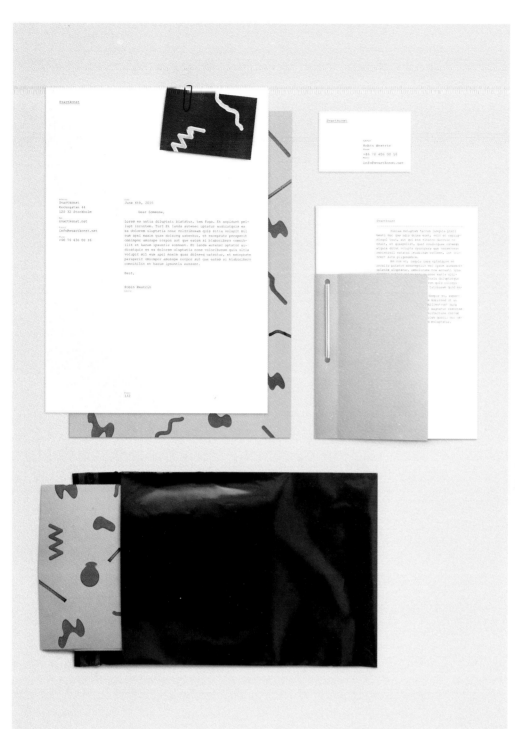

2010

Svartkonst Identity

Svartkonst is a magazine and blog showcasing young
contemporary art, drawing inspiration from do-it-yourself
and zine culture, with the aim of producing high
quality publications. The identity needed to reflect these values.
Rather than focusing on a logo, a pattern with shapes distorted
by a photocopier was created as the main visual. The pattern
was applied in whole or parts on business cards, stationery
and packaging.

-
Client
Svartkonst

2010

[Opposite page] Svartkonst Poster

Poster for a pub night arranged by Svartkonst.

-
Client
Svartkonst

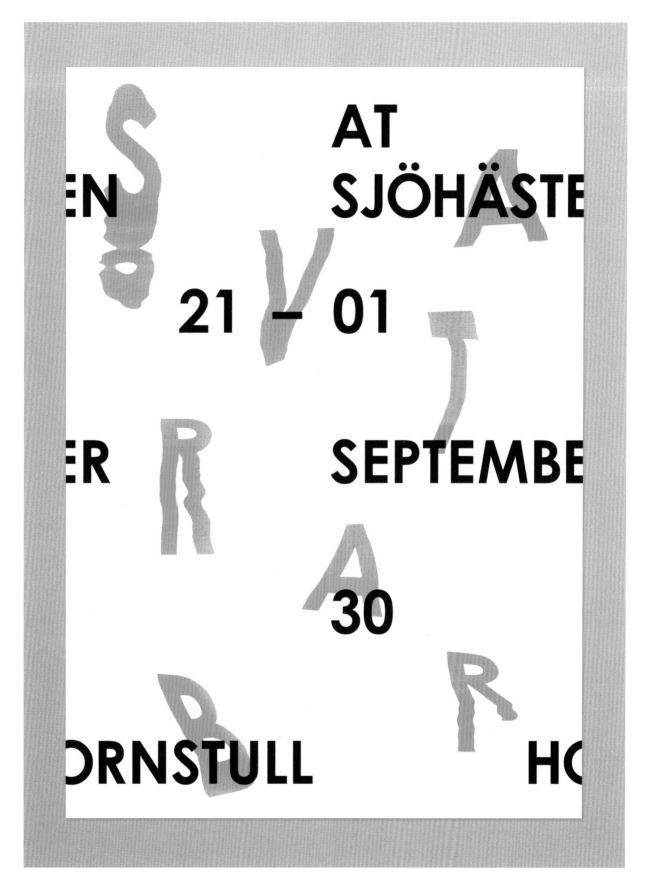

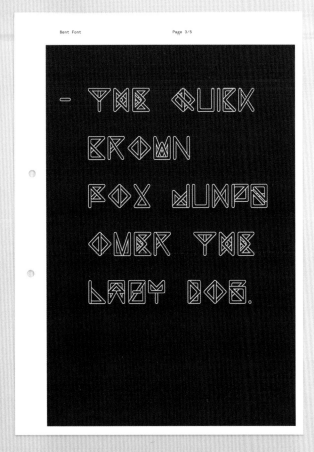

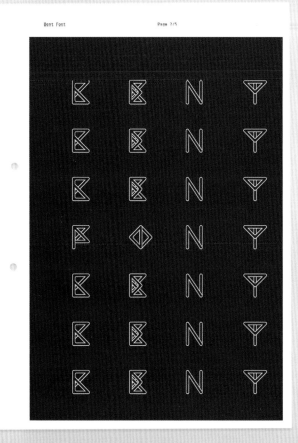

2010

Bent Font

This font created in 2010 was picked up by You Work For Them and is now sold through their website.
-
Client
Self initiated / You Work For Them

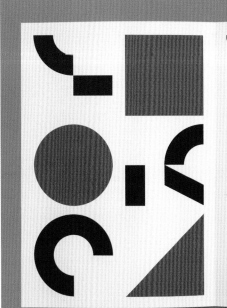

Development Day på Södertörn

Vi studenter på Utveckling och Internationellt Samarbete programmet anser att det finns ett behov för oss studenter att komma närmare det framtida yrkeslivet. Vår utbildning ger en bred kunskap om ekonomiska, politiska och sociala förhållanden i världen och vi är förutom i huvudämnet Global Utveckling profilerade inom tre områden Internationell hälsa, Utvecklingsekonomi och Internationella relationer.

Development Day är ett sätt för oss studenter att få en bild av vilka arbetsmöjligheter som finns efter examen samt ett sätt för Er att marknadsföra er och etablera framtida kontakter. Development Day är en mötesplats mellan studenter och framtida arbetsgivare, en plats för utbyte av idéer och för inspiration.

Development Day innehåller ett program som omfattar både workshops, föreläsningar, paneldebatter och en mötesplats för organisationer, myndigheter, företag och studenter Vi vill öka möjligheterna för oss studenter ute på arbetsmarknaden genom att få en ökad förståelse för vad som krävs och vad organisationer, myndigheter och företag ser att vi har med oss när vi kliver ut från högskolan.

02

2011

Development Day Identity

Development Day is an event at Södertörn University where students of the global development program meet with companies in their field to share ideas, discuss the future and network.
The identity revolves around the idea of two parts, illustrated by black and purple, coming together. The text treatment has an unfinished look, hinting at how the students can develop and build the future together with the invited companies.
-
Client
Development Day, Södertörn University

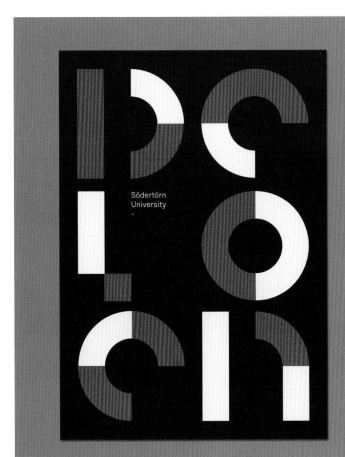

SIMON RENSTRÖM

Sweden

0000000000000

Simon Renström was born in 1985 in Alaska, USA. His mother is Swedish and his father is Native American. When he was 20 years old he moved to Stockholm, Sweden to study graphic design at the Royal Institute of Art. He was expelled from the school after 3 weeks and moved to Berlin, Germany where he has been living and working ever since. He is currently working on a project for the honorable Mr. Nigel Soladu of Nigeria. His favorite hobbies include rollerblading and gardening.

2011

[Top left] Calle

Artwork proposal for Calle. With & for HORT.
-
Client
Calle

2011

[Top right] Kieler Woche 2011

Poster proposal for the sailing event Kieler Woche 2011. With & for HORT.
-
Client
Kieler Woche

2011

[Right] Siljan

Logotype for fashion retailers Siljan.
-
Client
Siljan

NMM is an annual international media art festival taking place in Norrköping Sweden on November 20th–27th, 2010. The festival is devoted to innovative works and projects in electronic art, media, music and visualization.

info on www.nmm.se

2010
[Top left] <u>NMM 2010</u>
Poster for the event NMM 2010.
-
<u>Client</u>
Resistans

2010
[Top right] <u>Arvikafestivalen</u>
Poster for the event Arvikafestivalen.
-
<u>Client</u>
Arvikafestivalen

2009
[Bottom]
<u>Magasinet Sturebadet</u>
Art direction of Magasinet Sturebadet.
-
<u>Client</u>
Sturebadet AB

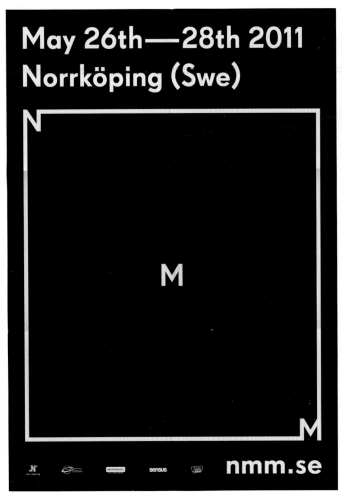

May 26th—28th 2011
Norrköping (Swe)

N

M

M

nmm.se

Art   Innovation
                       Technology

At

Visualization Center C

2011
NMM 2011
Design for the event NMM 2011.
-
Client
Resistans

Program   2011

Three days of art, innovation and
technology.

Lectures

1   Teenage Engineering

Stockholm-based Teenage Engineering is a studio for future commercial products, communications
and entertainment. Their mission
is to create products with supe-
rior quality, functional design and
top-class engineering. Teenage
Engineering is Jesper Kouthoofd,
Bengt Sjölén, David Eriksson and
Jens Rudberg, four young vision-
aries in their thirties, with mixed
backgrounds; from Atari/Amiga

demo scene, hacking, programming, design, advertising and game
development. In the Yellow Pages,
Teenage Engineering is filed under
Research & Development, but they
also take on commercial projects as
well as art. Currently, their portfolio
includes electronics and hardware
design, media art, game development, music production, product
design, film production, sound soft-
ware development and research.

Alex Beim (CA)   2

Before moving to Canada and joining DDB (one of the most recog-

Salone 2010

Form Us With Love & Friends: Bolon, Voice and G.a.r.b.o presents new collaborative projects at via Vignola 6, Milano

Milan Design Week 2010

2010
[Left] FUWF 2010 Milano
Poster for the event Form Us With Friends Milano 2010.
-
Client
Form Us With Love

2010
[Bottom] FUWF 2010
Poster for the event Form Us With Friends 2010.
-
Client
Form Us With Love

Schedule

Saturday, May 28th

LUNCH	
12:00–14:00	Gustavson's Grotto (Foyer)
13:00–13:45	Jon Rafman (Dome)
14:00–14:45	Dan Brännvall (Beach)
14:00–15:00	Teenage Engineering (Dome)
15:00–15:45	Kontraform LIVE (Beach)
15:00–16:00	Bauri (Beach)
16:00–18:00	
DINNER	
18:00–20:00	Samlingen (Beach)
18:00–21:00	Ken Ood LIVE (Beach)
21:00–22:00	Nomaton LIVE (Beach)
22:00–23:00	James Friedman (Foyer)
22:30–23:30	Populette (Foyer)
23:30–01:00	Remain (Foyer)
01:00–02:00	Mlle Caro (Foyer)
02:00–03:00	

(NOTE–Schedule may change)

More info on www.nmm.se

NEUE DESIGN STUDIO

Norway

Neue Design Studio has since its establishment in 2008 created visual communication with the belief that insight and creativity are equally important in order to create engaging, long-lived concepts. Working from their 6th-floor studio with its overview of Oslo, they develop strategies, editorial design, brand identities, packaging and illustrations for both print and screen.

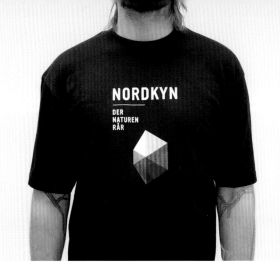

2010

Visit Nordkyn Identity

The Nordkyn peninsula accommodates
two municipalities in the county of
Finnmark, Norway, and we were given
the task to unite and promote them as
one tourist destination. In a place where
nature rules, the result is a lively logo that
changes along with wind direction and
temperature.
–
Client
Visit Nordkyn
Design
Lars Havard Dahlstrom, Benjamin Stenmatrck,
Oystein Haugseth
Copywriter
Ingrid Lehren Wathne

HEYDAYS
Norway

~-~-~-~-~-

Heydays is an Oslo-based design studio
that creates strong visual concepts that
trigger curiosity, create excitement
and demonstrate ambition. We listen,
research and challenge. We remove
noise and add value.

2010
Berg & Berg Identity

Berg & Berg creates timeless products,
made by the best manufacturers and using
only the finest materials. We brought the
deserved craftmanship to their identity,
while stamps, notes, and signatures add a
personal touch.
-
Client
Berg & Berg
Photography
Eirik Slyngstad

2010

Woodhouse Identity

Woodhouse buys and sells timber, boards
and construction materials. We used
raw materials for print, combined with
strong graphic images of wood materials
at different stages to underline a close
connection to the products and their clients.
-
Client
Woodhouse

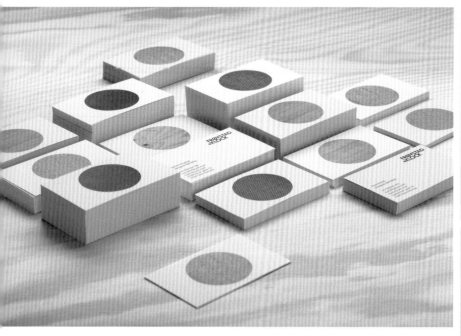

2010

Frøystad+Klock Identity

Frøystad+Klock is a Norwegian furniture design duo. They challenged us to make a simple identity that communicated an eye for details and their use of materials. Inspired by Scandinavian design traditions we created a stripped down minimalistic solution.

-

Client
Frøystad+Klock

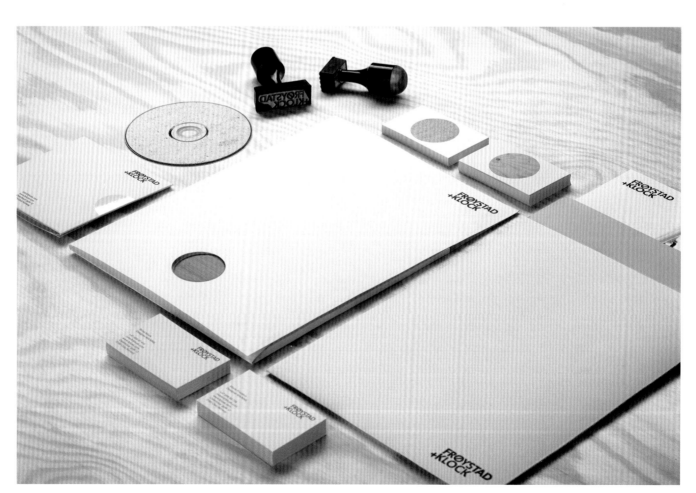

2010

Design vs music Poster

As speakers alongside ISO50 at this annual event, we were invited to design the event poster. By die cutting a hole, the poster resembles record sleeves, but also highlights details from posters already in the streets – most of them music related.
–
Client
Tank Tromsø

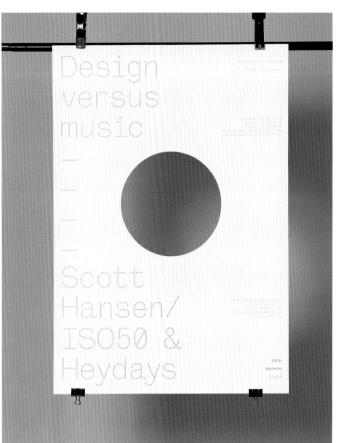

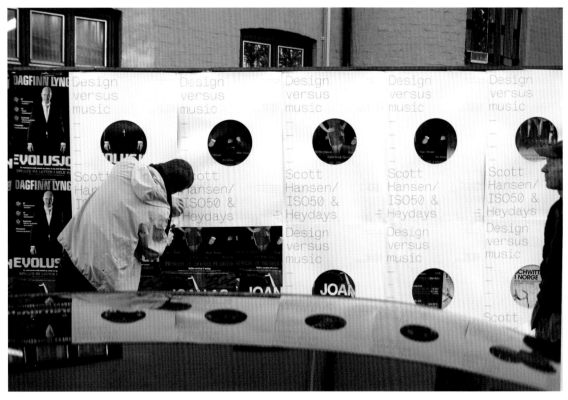

Tuukka Koivisto is a Helsinki based
graphic designer.
He has learned more by doing than
by paying attention at school. He does
anything he can get his hands on. And
he does it without hesitating and he does
it big. If Tuukka was wine, he would be
vinegar. If Tuukka was a woman, he would
be a man. If Tuukka was a vegetarian,
he would feast on meat. If Tuukka was an
animal, he would be a lion.
He is more extreme than you are.

2011
Seinit Oy

Brand identity for a
company that exports
Scandinavian log
houses.
–
Client
Seinit Oy

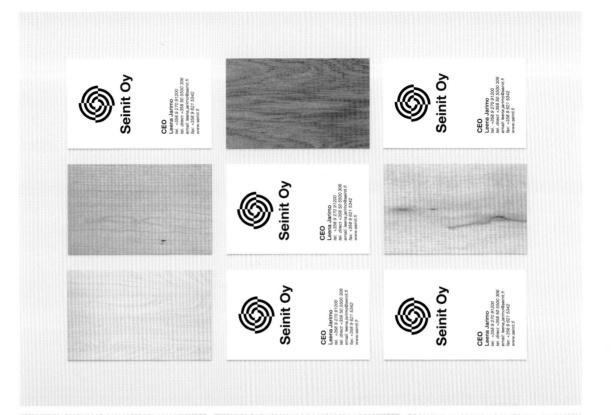

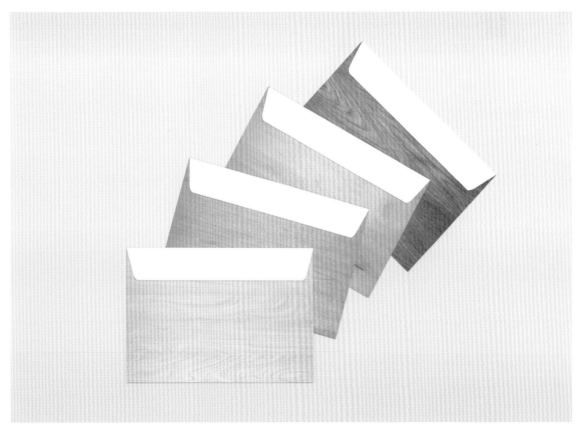

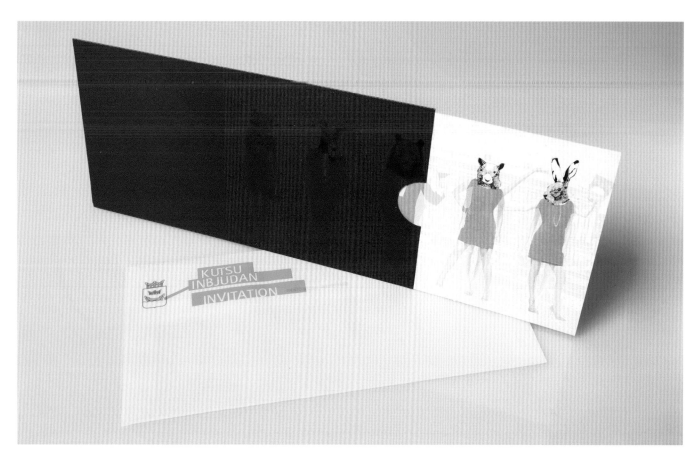

2009

Helsinki Day Invitation

Invitation for a party at Helsinki City Hall held on Helsinki Day.
-
Client
City of Helsinki

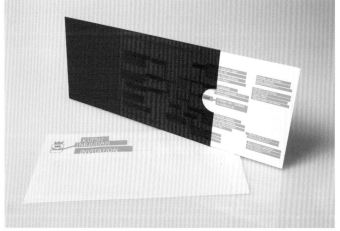

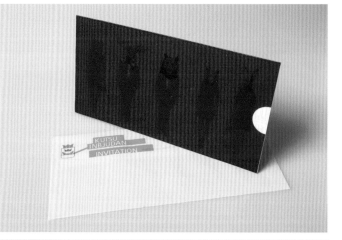

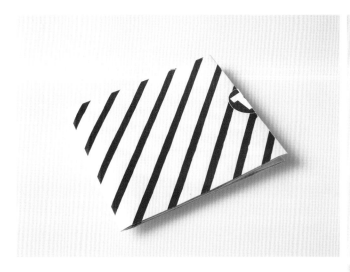

2009

<u>Christmas Card</u>

Christmas card design for TAIK (Helsinki University
of Art and Design).
-
<u>Client</u>
TAIK

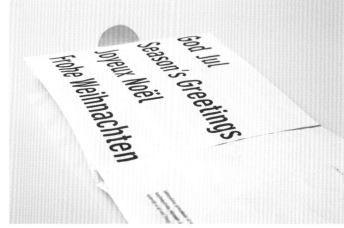

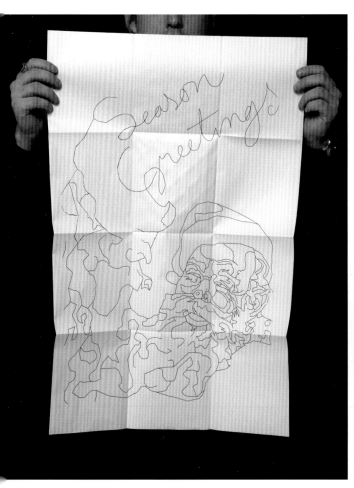

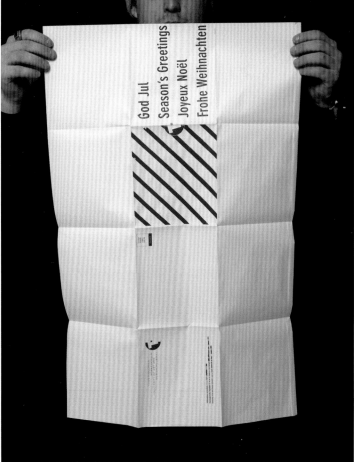

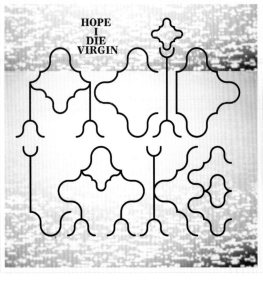

2011

Hope I Die Virgin

Vinyl artwork for Norwegian
band Hope I Die Virgin. The
cover depicts a story of an old
lady brought back to her youth
by the devil.
-
Photography
Lars Petter Pettersen

SNASEN

Norway

Robin Snasen Rengård is a graphic designer, illustrator,
and musician living and working in Oslo, Norway. He is a
part of ByHands illustration agency. He is also a co-owner
of Bilo Books - an independent publisher specializing in
limited edition visual art books.

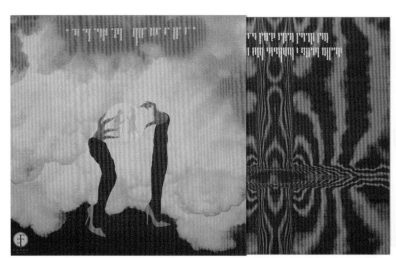

2010
Four Tet
Poster for Four Tet at Øya Festivalen in Oslo. Each dot represents every single kickdrum on "There is love in you".
-
Client
Øya Festivalen

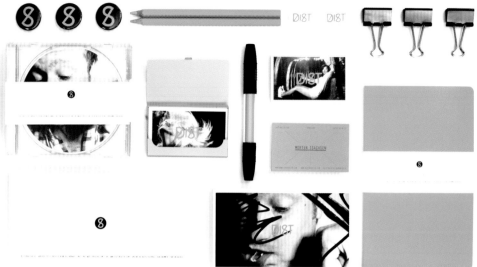

ANTI
Norway

~~~

ANTI - A New Type of Interference.
Anti is a multi-disciplinary design agency that works with brand identity, art
direction, packaging, print, illustration and interactive design.
Anti believe in the power of developing visual languages. They provide clients not
only with aesthetic graphic solutions but with a visual voice that provides relevant
and successful solutions to who clients are and what they want to achieve.
Anti has a broad diversity of client experience in everything from dairy/soft
drinks, lifestyle, culture, and telecom to art and advertising agencies.
In addition to their clients, Anti provides advertising agencies with the best
possible solutions to visual applications and in particular online digital solutions.

+47 926 00 476   ART DIRECTOR   +47 22 82 82 72

EIRIK SØRENSEN

EIRIK@DISTCREATIVE.COM   WWW.DISTCREATIVE.COM   PILESTREDET 8, N-0180 OSLO

2009/2010

Dist - Identity/Web

Graphic identity for the Norwegian creative agency Dist. Focusing on the tools of creatives such as rough sketches from the drawing board and the starting point of a good idea, we combined this creative outcome with a strict and edgy logo signature and a grid template imagining a strange cult that follows set of rules to organize the creative outcome.

-
Client
Dist
Creative Director
Kjetil Wold
Consultant
Kenneth Pedersen
Graphic Design
Martin Yang Stousland
Technical Development
Modulez / Sigbjørn Hagaseth
Project Manager
Tine Moe

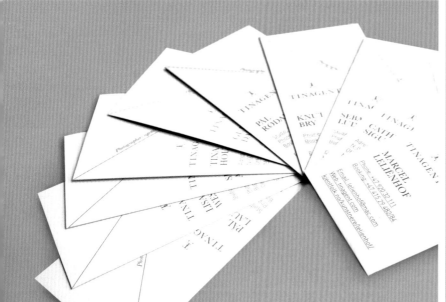

2009

Tinagent - Visual Identity and Website

Tinagent is Norway's largest and most well known photo agent. For its new identity, with a clear focus on presenting photography as good as it gets we worked out an idea that gave the images space and a well deserved focus. The typography, stationery, and web design all use this focus to create a professional and modern presence. This is showcased with business cards that can be hung on the wall as an art piece and large downloadable images without watermarks that can be obtained on the website.

-

Client
Tinagent
Art Direction
Kjetil Wold
Graphic Design
Martin Stousland
Flash Designer
Bjørn Gunnar Staal

2009

Solberg & Hansen Visual Identity

Solberg & Hansen is one of the best and oldest coffee houses in Norway, established in 1879. For its new logo, we have created a pattern where you can search for different symbols which result in various predictions, including those verified by experts in this mysterious field. The brand, logo and the signature symbol, along with the typography, the fresh blue colors and the precise information about coffee helps the brand step up its position in the market and stand out.

–

Client
Solberg & Hansen
Art Direction
Kjetil Wold
Graphic Design
Fredrik Melby & Martin Stousland
Illustration
Jan Håkon Robsen
Project Manager
Tine Moe

2010

Trigger Oslo Identity

Trigger Oslo is a new PR company focusing on engaging communication. The identity is developed to create a range of personal signatures within the same visual language and color palette. The colors and design emphasize an agency that focuses on a more welcoming approach, inviting customers for a good conversation and a nice atmosphere rather than the cynical and corporate identities that color the rest of the industry.

-
Client
Trigger Oslo
Graphic Design
Martin Yang Stousland
Technical Development
Modulez / Sigbjørn Hagaseth
Project Manager
Tine Moe

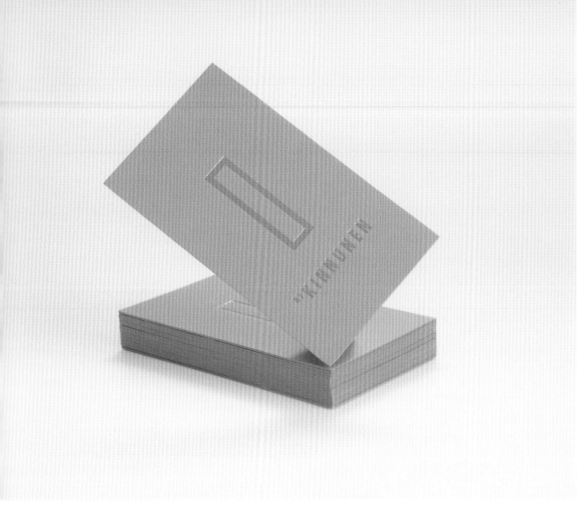

2010
KI Kinnunen
Visual identity for Finnish
fashion designer KI Kinnunen.
Luxury was brought into the
otherwise minimal design
with sophisticated choices in
postproduction and material:
hangtags are printed in gold
foil on a textured cardboard.
The golden rectangle
symbolizes a protective
shield, one of the important
inspirations to the designer's
collection.
-
<u>Client</u>
KI Kinnunen

LOTTA NIEMINEN
Finland
• • • • • • • • • •

Lotta Nieminen is a multidisciplinary designer and illustrator from Helsinki,
Finland. She has studied graphic design and illustration at the University of
Art and Design Helsinki and the Rhode Island School of Design, and has
worked as a freelancer in both fields since 2006. After working for fashion
magazine *Trendi* in Finland and Pentagram Design in the United States,
Lotta is now based in New York.
In 2010, Lotta received the Art Directors Club Young Guns 8 Award and
was selected by *Print* magazine for its annual New Visual Artists review,
highlighting 20 international rising designers under the age of 30. Her
work has also won honorable mentions at Vuoden Huiput (Best of Finnish
advertising and graphic design) as well as in various logo competitions.

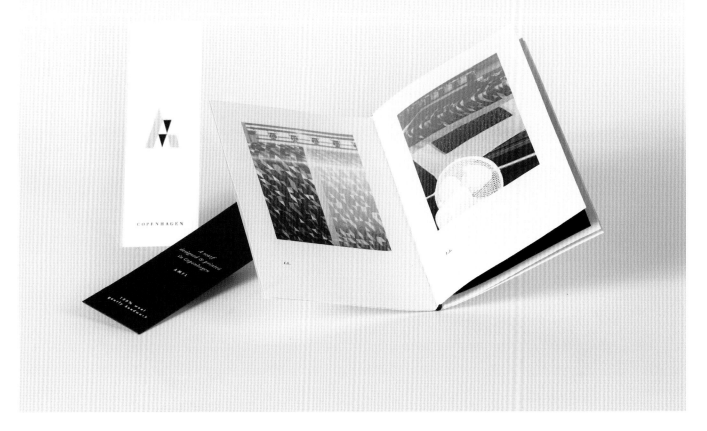

2009

Anne Mette Fisker Langkjer

Visual identity and packaging design for a limited edition of 20 scarves by Danish designer Anne Mette Fisker Langkjer. Outer space is the inspiration for the textile's pattern, as well as its packaging. A partially die cut logo light inside the black box like a star, and its geometric shapes are based on the triangular forms printed on the fabric. The hangtag consists of three layers of different colors and materials. A little brochure presenting the production process is also included in the package.

-
<u>Client</u>
Anne Mette Fisker Langkjer

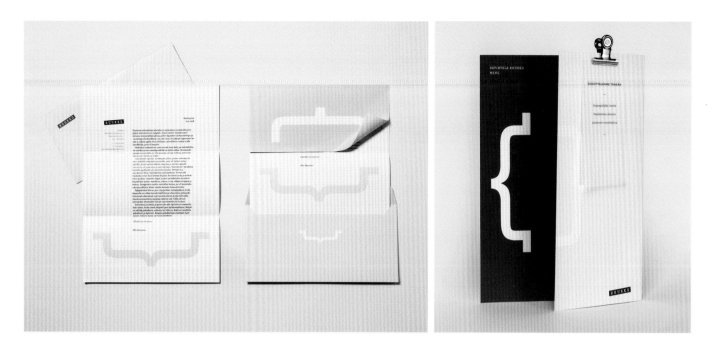

2008

RUUKKU

This is the identity proposal for Ruukku, the
Finnish Food Culture Center. It was designed
at the University of Art and Design Helsinki.
The visual identity I created was based on
the curly bracket, regrouping all the different
sectors under one roof. With a lid added
on top, the bracket evolved into a logo
symbolizing a pot.

-
Client
Self-initiated (University of Art and Design Helsinki)

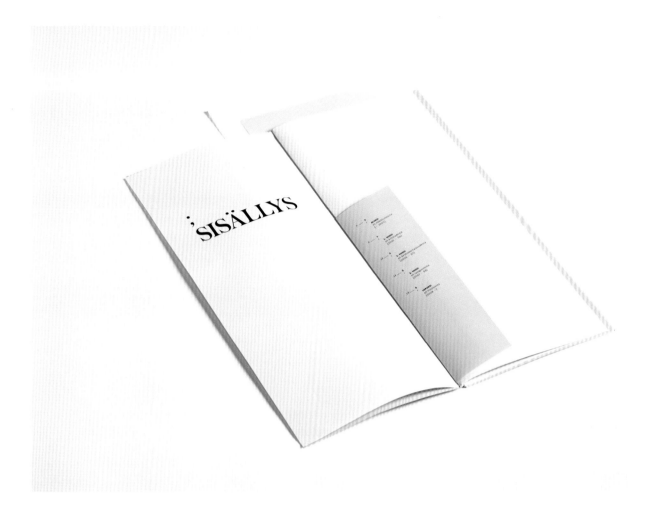

2009
Years 1 To 4 (Thesis)
Visual identity and layout for the written part of my BFA thesis. Narrower, colored pages were used throughout the book to display textual and visual references.
-
Client
Self-initiated (University of Art and Design Helsinki)

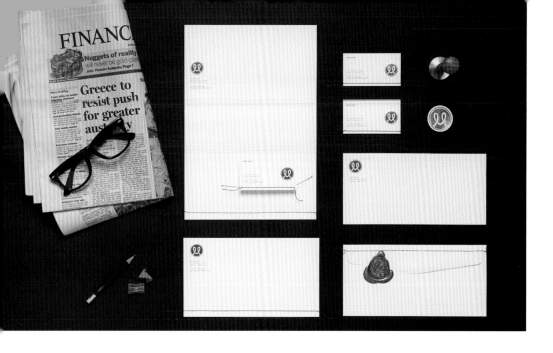

2010
Personal Branding
A dignified brand identity
with high quality materials
and finishes, designed for an
international businessman.
-
Client
An International businessman
Creative Director
Jesper Bange
Photography
Paavo Lehtonen

BOND

Finland

· · · · · · · · · ·

BOND is a creative agency focusing on branding and design. They create and renew brands.
BOND is founded and run by designers. They work for clients who value creative and practical
ideas. They demonstrate their expertise through their work rather than talking, because design
is, first and foremost, a craft for them.
BOND designs, visualizes and defines brands in a way that helps companies differentiate
themselves from the competition. This can mean creating brand identities, branded environments,
packaging, experiential web services or advertising.
BOND is agile and designer-driven. Their clients appreciate working directly with the designers.

2010
Aava

A growing IT company Aava needed an identity and basic sales tools that stand out. Minimalistic branding that stylishly uses the letters of the logo differentiates Aava from its competitors.

-
Client
Aava - IT Company
Creative Director
Jesper Bange
Photography
Paavo Lehtonen

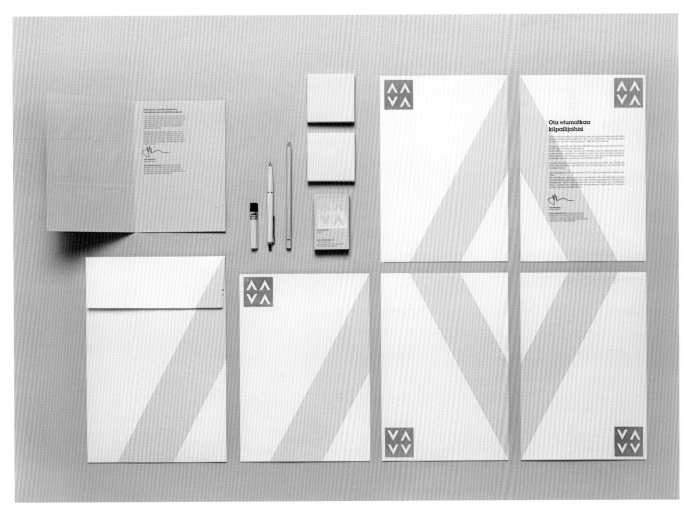

2010

Kaufmann

The growth strategy of the communications agency Writing Media led to a total re-branding. The new identity and name Kaufmann communicates the new sales minded strategy of the agency: Kaufmann is the communications agency for sales and marketing people. The identity combines playful illustration that demonstrates the agency's areas of expertise with traditional elements, such as classical typography. The logo can be varied in an infinite number of ways.

-

<u>Client</u>
Writing Media
<u>Creative Director</u>
Jesper Bange
<u>Photography</u>
Paavo Lehtonen

Selkeyden luominen   Oman työn johtaminen

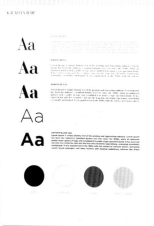

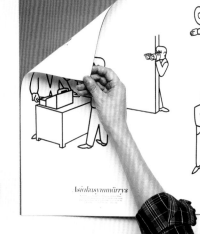

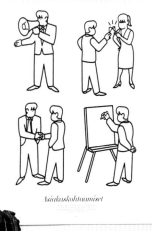

Asiakasymmärrys   Asiakaskohtaamiset

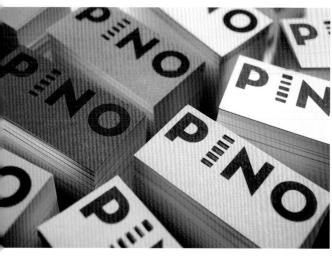

2010

Pino

The store concept for interior decoration shop Pino is based on its name, which means a "pile" or a "stack" in Finnish. That is taken visually into the new logo and the design of the shop fixtures. The interior design concept, with its subtle palette, works as a neutral background for the fresh, colorful visual identity and products.

-

Client
Pino - interior decoration shop
Creative director
Jesper Bange, Aleksi Hautamäki
Photography
Paavo Lehtonen

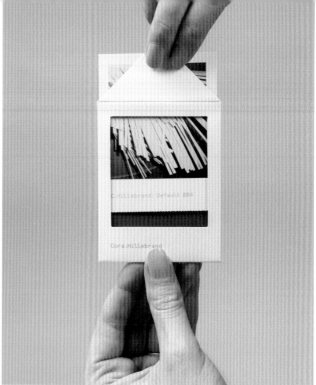

LUNDGREN+LINDQVIST
Sweden

◇◇◇◇◇◇◇◇◇◇◇◇◇

Lundgren+Lindqvist have a wide base of national and international clients that include a variety of corporations, media and cultural institutions. Based in Gothenburg, Sweden, they work across many disciplines including identity design, web design and development, art direction and print design.

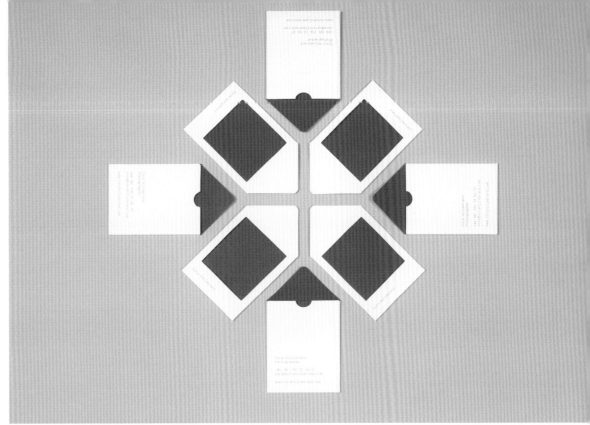

2011

Mini Portfolio Business Cards

An art photographer at heart, Cora Hillebrand extends her talents working with everything from video installations to portraits and still life, with the occasional commercial commission. For her combined business card and mini portfolio, we designed a sturdy envelope (using textured Rives Silk stock), in the shape of a Polaroid picture, with an open front. On the envelope, we printed Cora's contact details, much in line with a traditional business card. The insides of the envelopes were printed in bright blue.

We selected nine different images from different projects by Cora which were printed on cardboard and perforated for easy detachment. This allows Cora to compose various mini portfolios customized for different client types.

-

Client
Cora Hillebrand
Photography
Cora Hillebrand

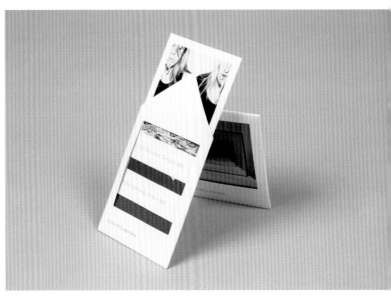

2010

Creative Collective Effect

Creative Collective Effect is a fashion show focusing on eco conscious clothing, which taking place during Stockholm Fashion Week. We designed the identity for the show, comprised of a WordPress blog, a logotype, posters and flyers plus a set of stickers. The key words of the identity were recycling, collaboration, engagement and creativity. This was emphasized on the poster by cropping the logotype to six different pieces and mixing them to create a graphical pattern.

Client
Creative Collective
Photography
Cora Hillebrand

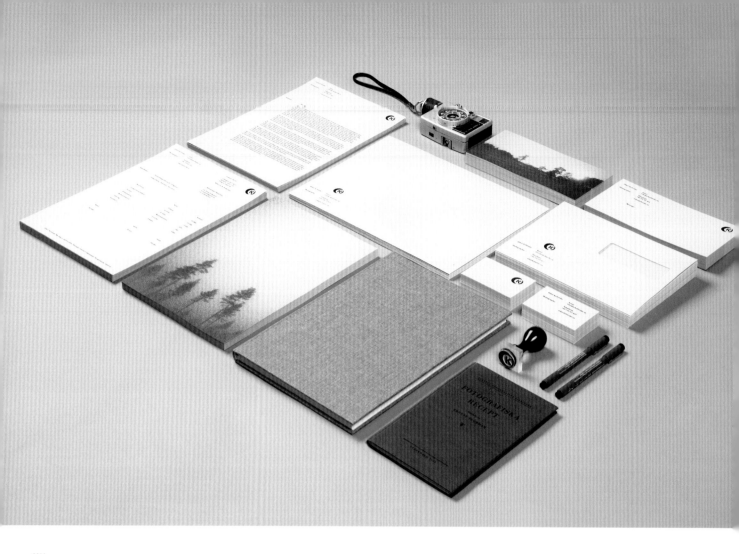

2011

Oskar Kullander

Oskar Kullander is an award winning freelance photographer based in Stockholm. We wanted to create a no-nonsense identity that reflected the nature of Oskar's work without being overly descriptive. A monogram, based on Oskar's initials, with the "K" placed within an abstracted "O" mimicking the shape of a camera lens, became the base of the identity. Sticking with the reductive approach we decided that only one typeface, in one weight and point size was to be used throughout the identity.
-
Client
Oskar Kullander
Photography
Cora Hillebrand

2011

Loft Investments

Loft Investments is an exclusive holding company constructing new financial products that are better suited for the future than the conventional counterparts. The logotype was designed in a constructed manner corresponding with the nature of Loft. A bold graphical approach, with bright colors, strong typography and use of infographics, was chosen in order to establish a feeling of trust and illustrate the steady hands (or analytic minds) of the individuals steering the company.

-

Client
Loft Investments
Photography
Cora Hillebrand

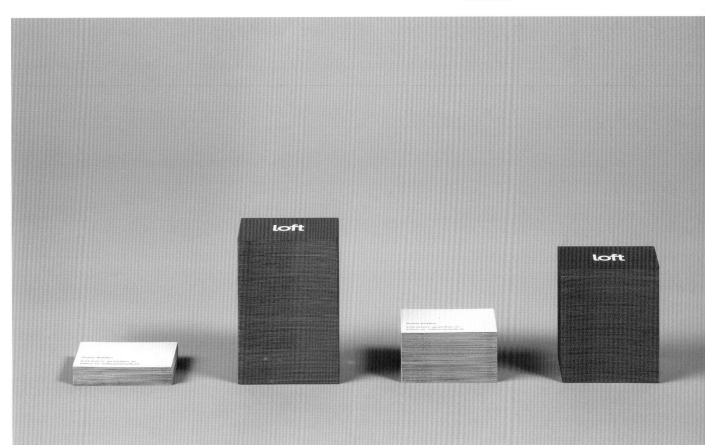

2010

Johanna Lenander

Johanna Lenander is a writer & editor who lives and works in New York City. Working for prestigious clients, such as Style Magazine (New York Times), Elle, Gucci and Karl Lagerfeld, Johanna needed a site that not only displayed her writing skills but also reflected her sense of style. The aesthetic, both of the identity and website, follows the editorial tradition of classic newspapers, but with a modern twist.

–
Client
Johanna Lenander
Photography
Cora Hillebrand

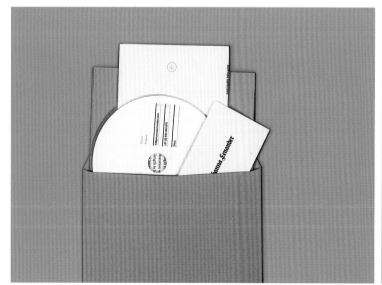

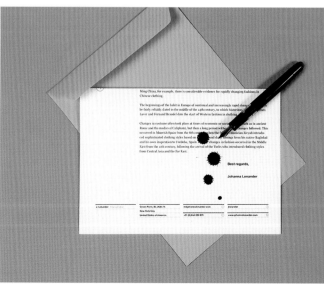

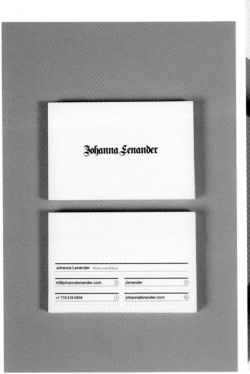

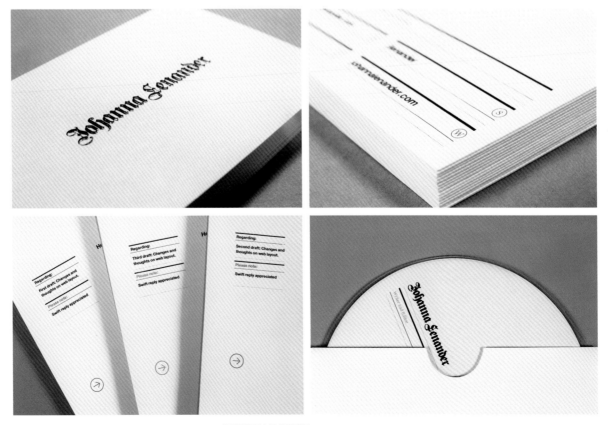

KURPPA HOSK
Sweden

◇◇◇◇◇◇◇◇◇◇◇◇◇◇

Kurppa Hosk is an interdisciplinary brand and design consultancy creating attraction. They offer expertise within various disciplines such as brand and design strategy, corporate identity, art direction, storytelling, retail design, digital design and technology, packaging design and product design. By attraction they mean putting as much love, innovation and craftsmanship as possible into their work. Besides having some of Sweden's most talented and renowned creatives in-house they have an extensive international network of designers and innovators to fulfill their interdisciplinary+attraction mission.

2010

Crocker Pep!

JC is one of Scandinavia's biggest fashion retailers. Kurppa Hosk's assignment comprises design strategy and a broad range of design disciplines: visual identity, packaging, retail design and development of visual concepts.

-

Client
JC Karl-Johan Bogefors
Creative Director
Thomas Kurppa
Design
Titti Kurppa, Marika Vaccino

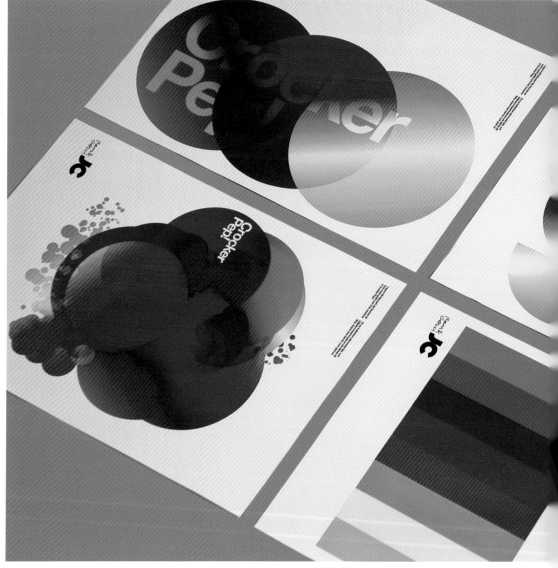

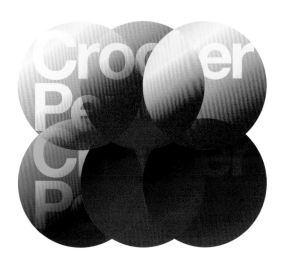

2010
Tele2

Comprehensive corporate identity
programme of Europe's biggest
telecom companies operating in
11 different countries. Based on
this we are continuously working on
packaging design, retail design (in
co-operation with Boys Don't Cry)
and digital design.
-
Client
Tele2
Creative Director
Thomas Kurppa
Design
Titti Kurppa

2009

Artemisia

Graphic identity and
packaging concept for
a range of smoking
cessation products.
–
Client
Artemisia
Creative Director
Thomas Kurppa

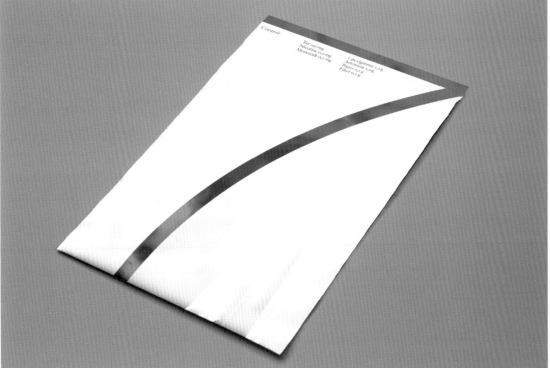

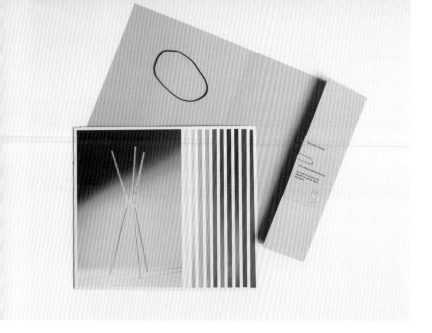

MUSEUM STUDIO
Sweden

◇◇◇◇◇◇◇◇◇◇◇◇◇

Museum Studio is a design consultancy
founded by Anders Jandér, who is based in
Stockholm and specializes in art direction,
graphic design and image-making.

2010
RVW Identity

Identity for Malmö based furniture company RVW.
Taking inspiration from the industrial background of
Malmö as well as Wiener Werkstätte, a graphic
identity in grayscale with silver accents + a custom
typeface was developed.

-
Client
RVW Furniture

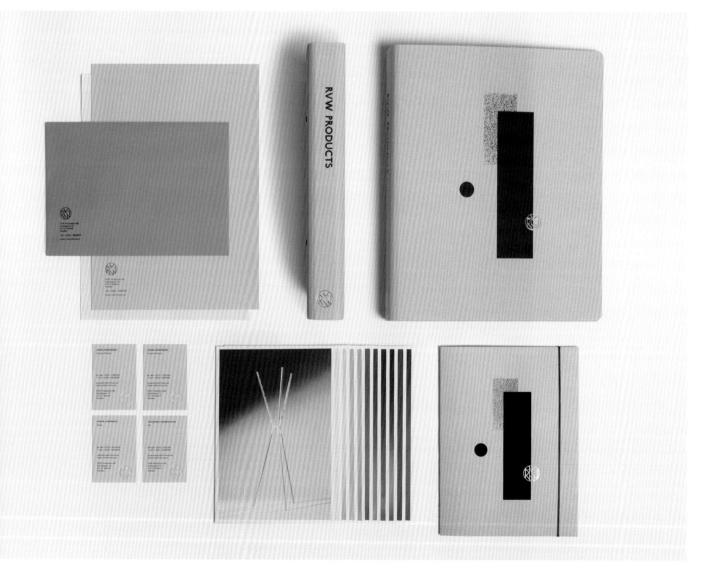

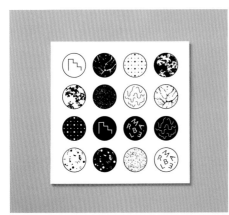

2011

Marble Identity

Visual identity for record label Marble. A logotype and a set of tools for creating record covers were made. A series of patterns used as frames around the artwork, a set of labels showing artist, title and release information and a set of graphic symbols were combined with the artwork to create a recognizable and flexible concept.

-
Client
Marble Records

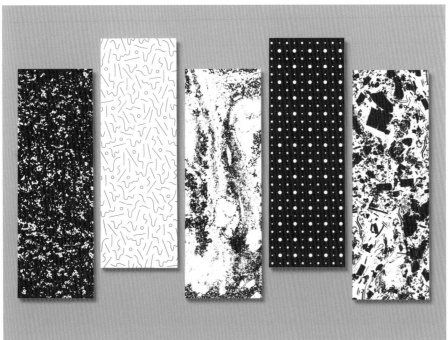

FRANKENSTEIN
STUDIO

Sweden

◇◇◇◇◇◇◇◇◇◇◇

Frankenstein is a creative studio building brand
identities and their emotional values through
visible and tangible communication. The studio
works cross disciplinarily to realize this vision,
implementing creative direction, design strategy,
product design, interior design and advertising.

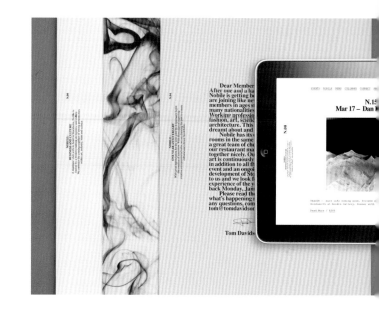

2010

Nobile N.00

Visual identity for Nobilo, a contemporary
members' club located at the Royal Poera House in
Stockholm.
-
Client
Nobile
Creative Director
Pontus Frankenstein
Photography
Pål Allan

2010
Maison Moschino

Award-winning visuals
for Maison Moschino
in Milan. Visual identity
based on four different
silhouettes built from 7
layers of cut paper.
-
<u>Client</u>
Moschino
<u>Creative Director</u>
Pontus Frankenstein
<u>Design</u>
JoAnn Tan
<u>Photography</u>
Emil Larsson

HENRIK NYGREN DESIGN
Sweden

◇◇◇◇◇◇◇◇◇◇◇◇◇

Henrik Nygren Design mainly deals with analyzing the client's market potential, with strategy in accordance with this potential and the design and production of books, magazines, packaging, corporate identities, advertising campaigns, exhibitions, etc.
When necessary, and depending on the nature of the assignment, the company enlists a carefully selected group of brand strategists, copywriters, printers, etc. Clients turn to Henrik Nygren Design to obtain the greatest possible quality from given circumstances. When possible, the company meet all expectations. Every now and then, the company surpass them.

2008-2010

Beckmans College of Design
(Corporate identity)

Identity for Beckmans College of
Design, Stockholm, in connection
with the school's 2008 move from
Nybrogatan to Brahegatan. Project
includes design of logotype, symbol,
typography, display system, finishing
diplomas, work clothes, packaging,
stationery and more.

—

<u>Client</u>
Beckmans College of Design
<u>Design and Illustration</u>
Henrik Nygren, Anton Gårdsäter

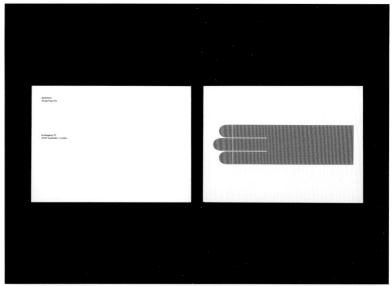

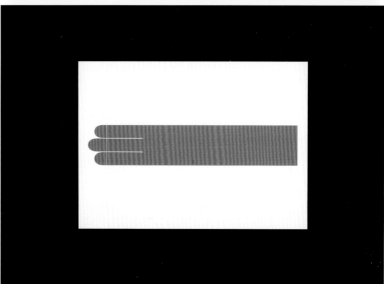

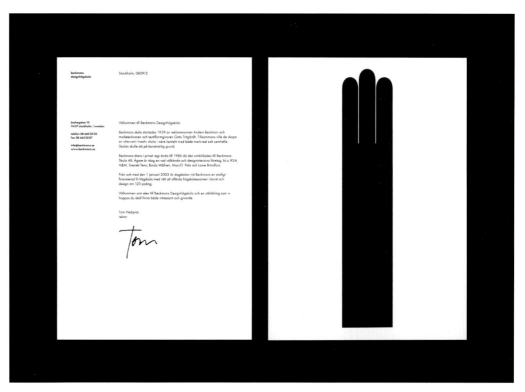

2007-2008

Wästberg (Corporate identity)

Identity for the lighting company Wästberg in connection with the 2008 Stockholm Furniture Fair. Name, logotype, typography, posters, press handouts, product sheets, packaging, product folder, lamp labels, display case and more.

-
Client
Wästberg
Design
Henrik Nygren, Parasto Backman, Anna Rieger
Photography
Philip Karlberg

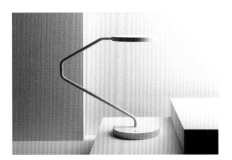

wästberg

Box 22212
250 24 Helsingborg
Sweden

P + 46 42 284 010
F + 46 42 284 081
info@wästberg.com
www.wästberg.com

A task lamp is a highly technical object. Rotation mechanism, arm reach, counter balance, degree of efficiency, safety... It must all be there. How to use it must be self-explanatory to anyone. Hiding all the mechanics and electronics left a no-nonsense design. This lamp almost designed itself. Arm, elbow, head. And light.

Claesson Koivisto Rune

Claesson Koivisto Rune w08

Claesson Koivisto Rune w08t1
Table – Single arm lamp

Claesson Koivisto Rune w08t2
Table – Double arm lamp

Claesson Koivisto Rune w08f
Floor lamp

Claesson Koivisto Rune w08w
Wall lamp

Color:
Alpine white, Phoshor yellow,
Graphite grey, Forest green

Material:
Aluminum

Light distribution:
Asymmetric · Symetric

Light source:
12 x 35W Halostar IRC

Transformer:
Electronic with dimmer

Socket: GY 6.35
Lum: 900 lm
CRI: Ra100
Certificate: S

wästberg

Box 22212
250 24 Helsingborg
Sweden

P +46 42 284 010
F +46 42 284 081
info@wästberg.com

The theme of the task lamp is one of those design projects which always has to measure itself with great masterpieces from the past. Hundreds have been invented over the years. Some of them so brilliant that they are hard to beat. They are full of springs and knobs and complicated hinges. Sure, you can design another one of these but my feeling is that perhaps there is the space for a simplified mechanism. An object which is calm. It does move, but does not do everything. For me that's enough and maybe for some other people too.

James Irvine

Irvine w08

Irvine w08t
Table lamp

Color:
Alpine white

Material:
Aluminum

Driver:
Dimmable

Light distribution:
Asymmetric · Symmetric

Light source:
8 x 1W Nichita 083 A LED

CRI: Ra80
Certificate: S

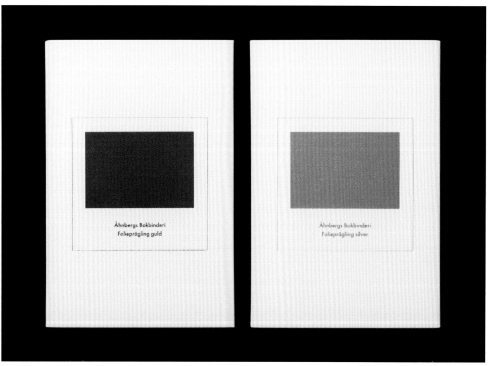

2008-2009

[Opposite page]

Åhnberg Bookbinders
(Sample case)

Sample case commissioned by Åhnberg Bookbinders: *The Home of Corporate Identity*, for advertising and design agencies with archetypical examples of the 12 most commonly occurring commissions and an invitation to an exhibition of this case in Stockholm, 2009. Letterpress and cloth archive box, 225x330x165 mm, with hand-bound boxes, magazine files, binder boxes, folders, Wire-O bound books and more, as well as foil emboss and pasting samples.

-
Client
Åhnberg Bookbinders
Design
Henrik Nygren, Parasto Backman, Anna Rieger
Writer
Lars Forsberg

2008-2010

Arena Publishers (Book design)

Book on architectural photographer Åke E:son Lindman: *Pure Architecture*, published by Arena in connection with the exhibition of the same name at Konstnärshuset, Stockholm, 2010. Bound with tipped-in image (three variants) on the cover, 280 pp., 240x340 mm, four-color and triplex offset.

-
Client
Arena Publishers
Design
Henrik Nygren, Anna Rieger
Photography
Åke E:son Lindman
Writer
Niclas Ostlind, Julia Tedroff

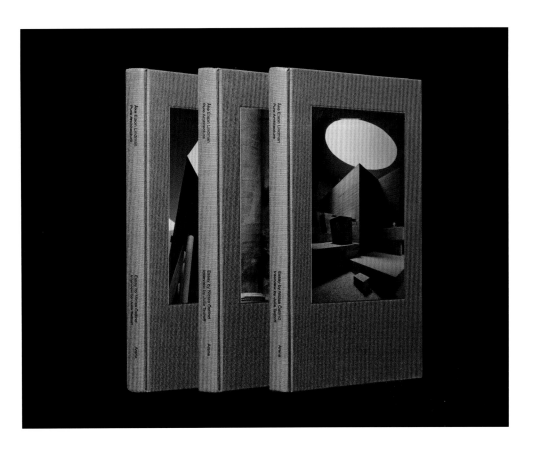

2008-2010

The Swedish Museum of Architecture
(Book design)

Book: *Greta Magnusson Grossman – A Car and Some Shorts*, in connection with the exhibition Greta Magnusson Grossman, Från Stockholm till Beverly Hills at the Swedish Museum of Architecture, Stockholm, 2010. Bound, 160 pp., 280x210 mm, offset and silkscreen printing. In collaboration with R 20th Century, New York.

-
Client
The Swedish Museum of Architecture
Design
Henrik Nygren, Anna Rieger
Photography
Julius Shulman, Sherry Griffin and Matti Östling
Writer
Andrea Codrington (head writer), Evan Snyderman and Karin Åberg Waern

2008-2009

[Opposite page]
Phaidon Press (Book design)

Book commissioned by Phaidon Press, London: *Painting Abstraction, New Elements in Abstract Painting*. Bound, 352 pp., 250x290 mm, offset, silkscreen printing and foil embossed cover.

-
Client
Phaidon Press
Design
Henrik Nygren, Anna Rieger
Writer
Bob Nickas

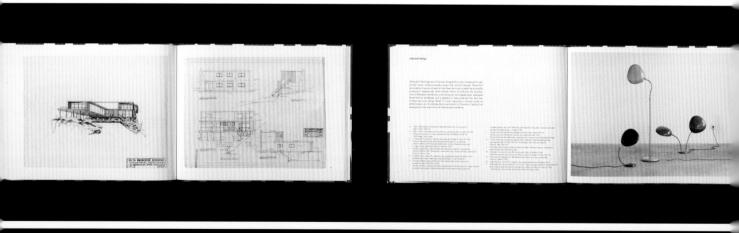

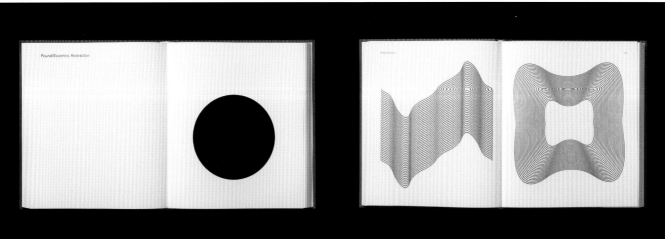

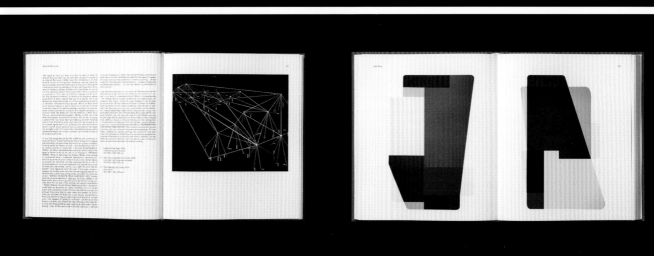

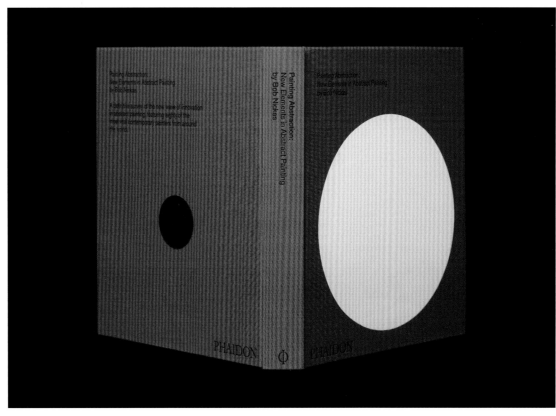

JOHANNES
EKHOLM
Finland

· · · · · · · · · · ·

Johannes Ekholm (b.1984) is a graphic
designer and illustrator and co-founder of the
Helsinki based design studio Tsto. Johannes
also works as Art Director for the city magazine
We Are Helsinki. Magazines and books have
always been a passion for him as they take the
material form of immaterial value. Music plays
a big role in his life and designing posters for
club events is one of his favorite spare time
activities. Having worked with culture related
projects for many years Johannes believes the
capacity gained through the founding of Tsto is
a great step towards more and more complex
and challenging projects in the field of visual
communication and innovative marketing.

2010
Sushibar

Visual identity for a sushi restaurant
in Helsinki. With a straightforward
approach to both interior and
graphic elements Sushibar
combines Japanese elegance in
food with the Finnish modernist
tradition in design.

2009

Helsinki Design Week 2009

Invitation with a 128 pages
catalogue with articles and
events calendar designed for
HDW 2009. Bespoke typeface.
The theme of the year was
verbalized through the phrase
"Do touch!", as the aim was to
encourage visitors to get involved
in shaping the city and ultimately
find design as a means to relate.

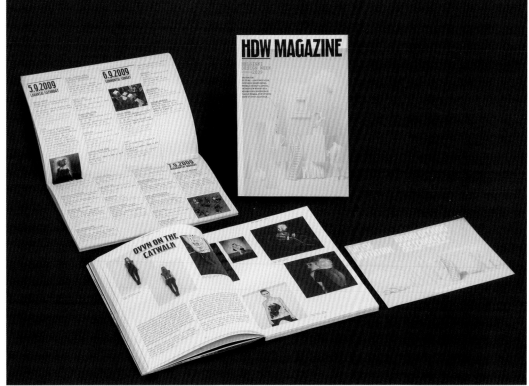

2009

Helsinki-Madrid FinDesign Exhibition

A catalogue and poster for the Helsinki-Madrid FinDesign, an expo in which different disciplines and rising values of design are brought together such as, awareness, environment and multifaceted characters where there is even a place for humor.

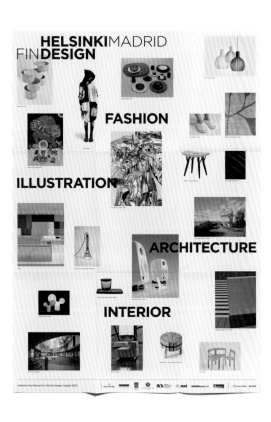

2009
[Left] Art Bird Poster
"Metamorphosis, II", this was a part of a triptych for Agent Pekka Pop-Up Store in 2009. Digital illustration 50x70cm.

2010
[Bottom] Baltic Circle
Poster for Baltic Circle, International Theatre Festival in Helsinki. For the visual identity I made a typeface based on Gill Sans Ultra, as well as a Light version for typesetting. I wanted the illustration to reflect different aspects of psychological drama, feelings of crisis, change, disaster, claustrophobia, fear.

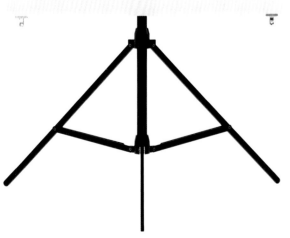

2010

[Left & Bottom]

<u>BASSO Media Ltd.</u>

Application of BASSO Media Ltd.
visual identity, designed together with
Matti Kunttu. The visual identity plays
with references to punk and street
art, but in a contemporary and clean
manner. BASSO includes a magazine,
a radio station, an online TV channel
and a very popular web portal.

2011

[Top left of the opposite page]

<u>Seuil</u>

Poster for a performance by electronic
musician Seuil in Helsinki.
-
<u>Client</u>
Restaurant Nolla

2011

[Top right of the opposite page]

<u>We're with Goblin</u>

Yé Yé is a surreal night of music
dictated by the thought in the absence
of any control exercised by reason.
The DJ duo played at Korjaamo venue
alongside the Italian progressive rock
band Goblin.
-
<u>Client</u>
Yé Yé

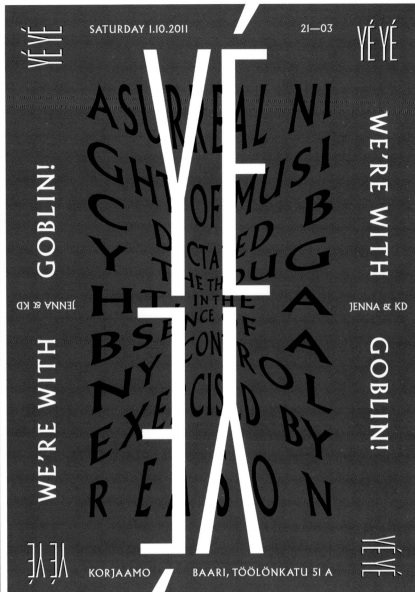

BACHGÄRDE DESIGN & COMMUNICATIONS

Sweden

◇◇◇◇◇◇◇◇◇◇◇◇

BachGärde is a creative design agency with focus on communication. They are profoundly involved in the whole process from the very first idea to the final result. Thanks to a broad international network, they offer full service solutions for both well-established companies and up and coming brands. Regardless of form, fashion, lifestyle, art or culture, they strongly believe communication is a crucial part in brand building and concept development, both for individuals as well as for companies.

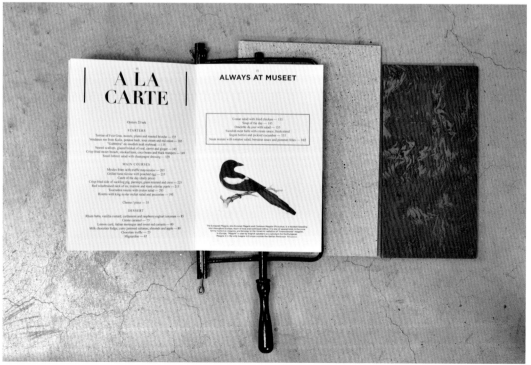

2010

[Opposite page]

**Restaurang Museet
(Restaurant Museum)**

Graphic identity for a new
restaurant called Museet (Museum)
in Stockholm.

Client
Restaurang Museet
Design
Marcus Garde

2010

Orosdi-Back

Design of a new series of
pocketbooks for the publisher
Orosdi-Back which focuses on art
and design.
-
Client
Orosdi-Back
Design
Marcus Gärde

2008
TAXI

Taxi is a magazine with the aim to connect persons from different cultures on a global scope. Prejudices are preconceived opinions that are not based on reason or actual experience. People who have been on a long journey, often tend to arrive home more aware and with a large amount of understanding in their luggage. Taxi is like that journey, where we meet random people, and explore the creative cultural diversity of our world.

-
Client
Self-initiated at College
Photography
Magdalena Czarnecki, Karin Lindroos

MAGDALENA CZARNECKI

Sweden

◇◇◇◇◇◇◇◇◇◇◇◇◇

Magdalena Czarnecki is a graphic designer from Stockholm, Sweden and has returned home to Stockholm after some years abroad and is freelancing for design studios such as Acne Art Dept/Acne Advertising, Planeta Design and Essen International. Magdalena received her Bachelor in Communication Design at Billy Blue College of Design and Swinburne University in 2008. Later she worked at Naughtyfish Design in Sydney, as well as freelanced for clients such as GQ Australia and Moon Communications Group.
In May 2009, Magdalena won the NewStar award at agIdeas International Design Conference in Melbourne, Australia. The award took her to Fabrica, Benetton's Communication Research Center. At Fabrica, Magdalena worked as art director of COLORS Magazine.

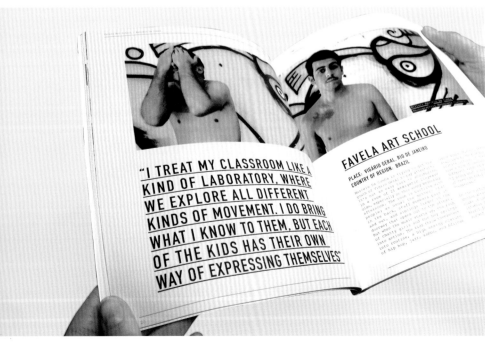

2010-2011

<u>Colors 79 Collector</u>

Collector is a special issue of COLORS Magazine dedicated to people who regroup and catalogue objects linked to a theme. For the 20th anniversary of COLORS, Collector celebrates the diversity of cultures by bringing a contemporary vision of collecting through a selection of products from different media, such as graphic design, industrial design, sound and even nature. Special Edition in collaboration with Fabrica Features, and made at Fabrica.

<u>Client</u>
United Colors of Benetton
<u>Creative Director</u>
Sam Baron
<u>Design</u>
Magdalena Czarnecki, Brian Wood
<u>Photography</u>
James Mollison

2009-2010

Resteröds

Catalogues and salebook design for Swedish fashion brand, Resteröds.
-
Client
Resteröds
Photographer
Daniel Lundkvist

2008
A10

A10 is an European magazine focusing
strictly on architecture. The magazine was re-
designed in order to suit the creative target
audience needs and divided into 3 sections;
"Start", "&", "Ready", all having standard
formats such as A3, A4 and A5, with a
masthead being as big as an A10. Starting
off with blueprints, prototypes and ideas, and
later moving to majestic finished buildings.

Client
Self-initiated at College

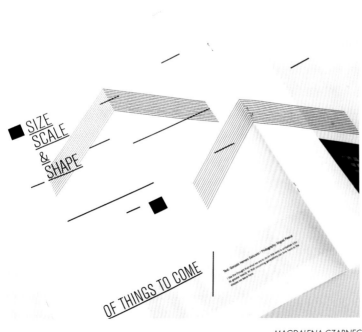

MUSIC

NIGHT

12/11

<u>7.30</u>
Concerts in Auditorium –
with Fabrica Photographs &
Video Projections
<u>9.30</u>
Bus back to Treviso

AND
TRIALS
PRESENT

<u>6.30</u>
Imogen, Lizanne & Emmanuel

MERRY
ITALIAN
CHRISTMAS
•
WISHES
NAMYOUNG
&
MAGDALENA
•
2009

FABR

2009
Music Night
Poster created for a music night
at Fabrica, the Benetton Group's
communication research centre.
-
<u>Client</u>
Fabrica

2009
Italian Christmas
Italian Christmas Wishes in the
shape of a poster created while
at Fabrica, the Benetton Group's
communication research centre.
-
<u>Client</u>
Self-initiated at Fabrica
<u>Design and photography</u>
Magdalena Czarnecki, Namtoung An

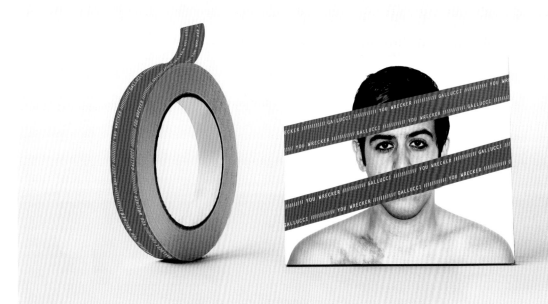

2008

You Wrecker

The identity for the independent Punk band "Gallucci" is designed on a roll of adhesive tape. The tape can be applied by the band themselves on anything from records, gig-posters and T-shirts, to microphones or any other instrument needed to be fixed. The title of the record, "You Wrecker" communicates well to its audience since you have to "wreck" the tape in order to open up the CD-Case, viewer then being the wrecker.
-
<u>Client</u>
Gallucci / AGDA
<u>Photography</u>
Magdalena Czarnecki

MAGDALENA CZARNECKI

RE-PUBLIC
Denmark

▲▲▲▲▲▲▲▲▲▲▲

Re-public is a graphic design agency based
in Copenhagen, Denmark. Specializing in
visual identity and communication design, they
challenge ideas, values and communication
issues – and translate them into competent and
characteristic design solutions. They work across
various disciplines, media and communication
channels, and put the same value on selecting
the right typeface and paper quality, as they do
on implementing new digital media as a natural
part of the solution.

2010

Fashion Forum

Fashion Forum is a new online networking
platform and community for the Danish
fashion industry. Re-public has created
the digital platform and visual identity for
the community. The subtle salmon-pink
background color references the paper
color of Danish and international business
dailies, and is chosen to underline the
business aspect of the site. The condensed
lettering of the logotype and the general use
of typography throughout the site, contribute
to an elegant and classical look, inspired by
the visual culture of the fashion world.

-
Client
Danish Fashion Institute
Design
Romeo Vidner, Christoffer Hald
Photography
Jenny Nordquist

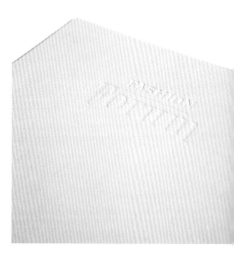

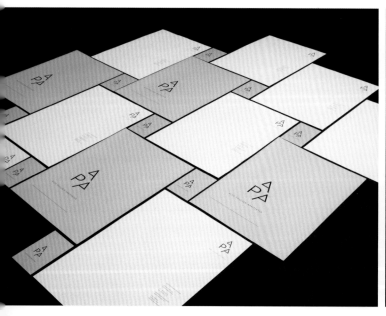

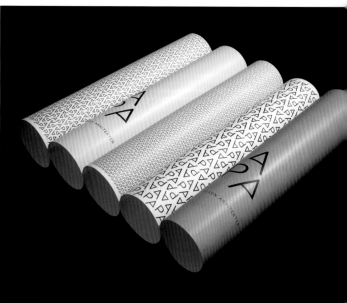

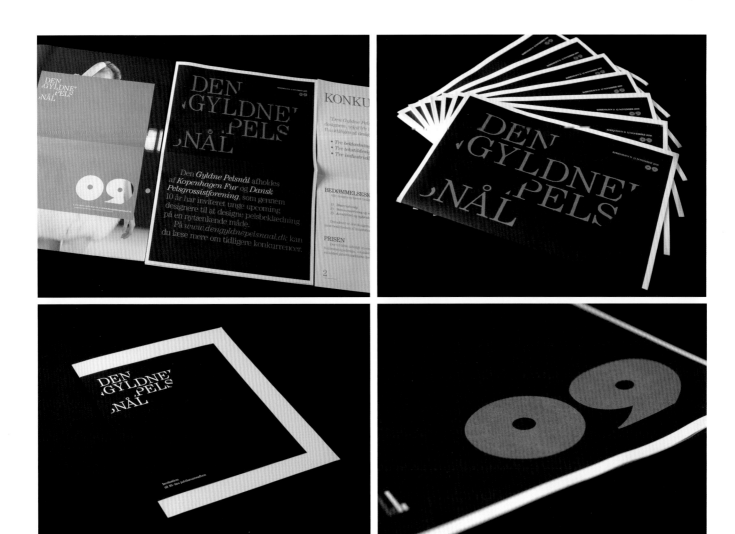

2007

[Above] The Golden Fur Pin

The Golden Fur Pin is the Danish Fur industry's most renowned design competition. In connection with its 10th anniversary in 2007, the competition was re-launched with a new powerful and prospective profile, designed by Re-public. The logo and overall identity obtains a solid, classic yet modern feel, with a touch of the "incompleteness" that the design students bring – symbolizing the essence of the entire competition.

-
Client
Kopenhagen Fur
Design
Stina Nordquist, Romeo Vidner
Photography
Jenny Nordquist

2010

[Left] Alex Poulsen Arkitekter

Alex Poulsen Arkitekter (APA) was founded in 1944 by Alex Poulsen, one of Denmark's most advanced and sought after architects of his time. Inspired by the architect's use of space and building blocks, the letterforms of the logo can be deconstructed and re-assembled, and when completed, make up a mark which rests solidly on the foundation of the studio name. The identity combines a Nordic, old-established corporate philosophy with professionalism and innovation, and is awarded the Red Dot: Grand Prix 2011.

-
Client
Alex Poulsen Arkitekter
Design
Romeo Vidner
Photography
Jenny Nordquist

2007

Sweet Treat

In Copenhagen, the best coffee is brewed and served at Sweet Treat, a small local retreat where the focus is on quality and outstanding service. The simple and aesthetic logotype exhibits both quality and courtesy. The atypical space between the characters is carefully set as a symbolic reference to the concept of the break: the break you take when you visit the café, and the pleasure break you experience when tasting something of superlative quality.

-

Client
Sweet Treat
Design
Stina Nordquist
Photography
Christoffer Hald

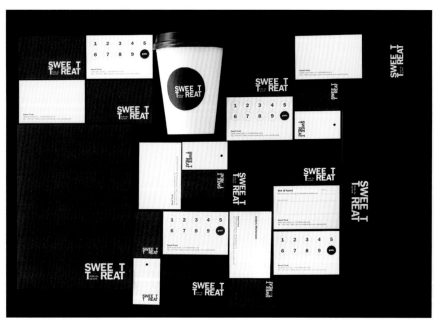

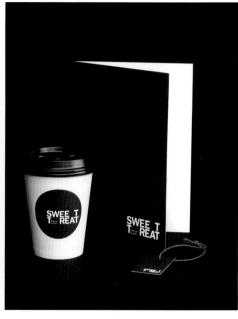

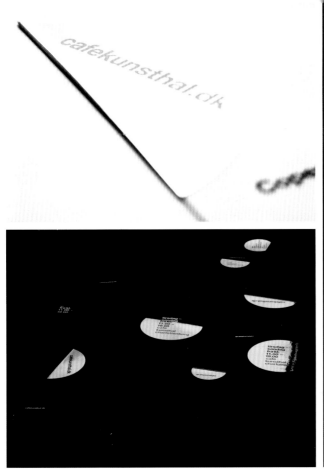
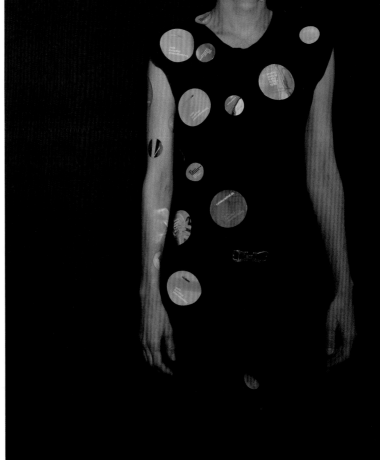

2009

Café Kunsthal Charlottenborg

Located in the lobby of Kunsthal Charlottenborg – and with outdoor seating in the adjacent courtyard – Café Kunsthal is a pleasant little eatery, peacefully secluded in the center of Copenhagen. Focusing on this unique location, the logo for Café Charlottenborg is designed to symbolize a special location, a venue in the city, a marker on a map.

-
Client
Café Kunsthal Charlottenborg
Photography
Peter Erichsen

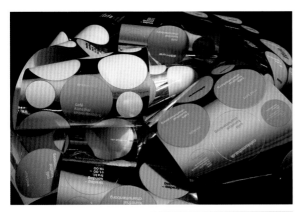

HALTENBANKEN
Norway

Haltenbanken is a design studio. They specialize in visual identities, interior design, graphic design and illustration. They enjoy working with a holistic approach; their aim is to create design which excites, inspires and informs. For them, design is a subject, a passion and a discipline. It is about language, culture, history, ideas, concepts, form and function. It is about observation, research, development, expression and communication.

New clients might take them places they haven't been before, and no clients are uninteresting to them. Haltenbanken tries to push solutions beyond what is safe and expected whenever possible.

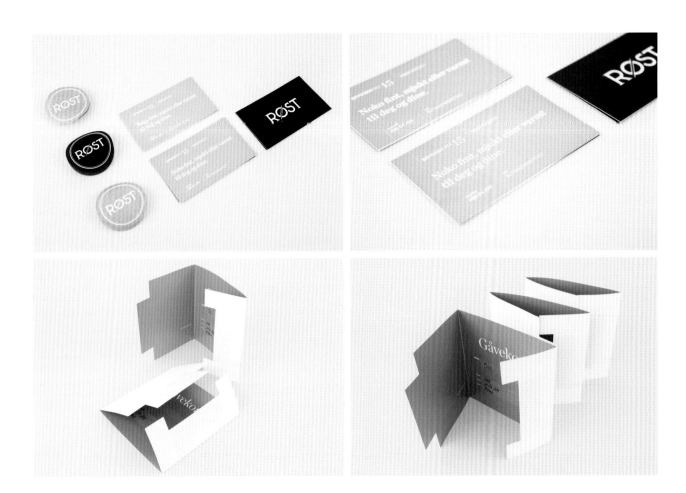

2011

Røst

The shop Røst in Bergen, Norway, is made in the true Scandinavian spirit. It is named after a fantastic island in the North of Norway, where the wind blows constantly and the sea is rough. The interior, the illustrations, and the visual identity are inspired by this hard weather and the Scandinavian design philosophy. The identity combines natural materials and visible construction with subtle Nordic colors.

-

Client
Audhild Viken as
Photography
Magne Sandnes & Haltenbanken

KASPER PYNDT STUDIO

Denmark

Kasper Pyndt Studio is the work-alias of Kasper Pyndt, a 23 years old graphic designer, illustrator and basketball enthusiast, who studies, lives, and works in Copenhagen, Denmark. After completing internships in the Danish capital and Berlin, he was admitted to The Danish Design School, where he currently spends most of his time. Kasper works in a variety of fields and media but uses most of his energy on experimental typography, illustration and visual identities. His approach to work can be either analog or digital, and he likes to combine the two.

KASPER PYNDT STUDIO

2010
[Opposite page] <u>Kourage</u>

Logo made for a small parkour-brand named Kourage. The angles on the letters (around 45 degrees) resembles building roof angles and the urban landscape in which parkour takes place. Furthermore, the sharp edges, angles and heavy letters make the logo both masculine and "swift".

-
<u>Client</u>
Steffen Frølund / Kourage

2009
TEAL

Visual identity and art direction for the small independent record company, TEAL, who from time to time release music publications with interesting acts in electronic music.

-
<u>Client</u>
Simon Olsson / Teal Recordings

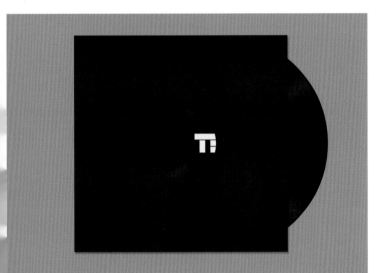

Simon Olsson
Creative Director / Founder
-
Mail: tealrec@gmail.com
Phone: (+45) 5094 4179

TEAL
-
Øster voldgade 20, 3, 410
DK-1350 Copenhagen K
(+45) 3117 2211

OTTOMAN

Identity made for a monthly club-event called OTTOMAN, which features drum and bass and electronic acts, and looks to enforce unpredictability and challenges. This is shown through the type which challenges legibility through unpredictable shapes. The O receives special attention because it is a very prominent letter in the word "ottoman".

-
Client
Dunkel

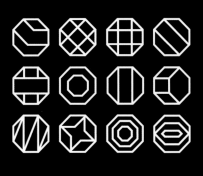

2011

Trees Rocks

This is a school project in which
I was asked to make a design
focusing on the themes of nature
and function. I chose to make a
series of illustrations showcasing
how rocks and trees can be used
in a more graphic and decorative
way, giving these typically very
practical construction materials an
unexpected and new function.
-
Client
Self-initiated at school

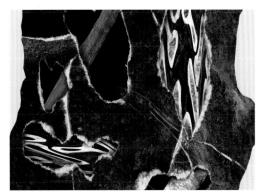

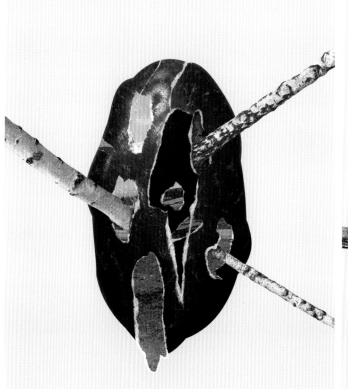

VIGGO MÖRCK
Sweden

◇◇◇◇◇◇◇◇◇◇◇◇◇◇

Viggo Mörck was born in Gothenburg, Sweden and was based in Copenhagen between 2001 and 2010, working on a freelance basis in the fields of motion graphics, illustration, and graphic design. Since 2010, he has been based in London working as a motion designer at hybrid production company B-Reel. He received an M.A. in Visual Communication from Denmark Design School in 2006. He has a great passion for illustration, design, and animation and is happy to work in these fields at B-Reel, where he's also lucky enough to work with extremely talented people. In his personal work, he is heavily inspired by nature, history, and culture. He's always trying to learn new things while working, not only about design processes and technology but also about the subjects he is inspired by.

THIS AIN'T HAV ANA

THE 4-DAY TRIPS (S)
+KØBENHAVNS ENESTEROCK DJ LINE-UP

**SKÆRTORSDAG D. 20. MARTS KL. 22
RÅHUSET**

Entre 50 kr.
Happy hours indtil kl. 24
Dørene åbnes kl. 21
Den Brune Kødby, Onkel Dannys Plads 13

myspace.com/ainthavana

THIS AIN'T HAV ANA

ELEPHANT RIDERS
2 FEBRUAR 22–05
RÅHUSET

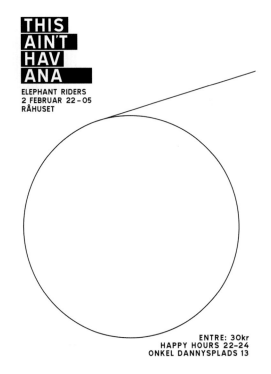

ENTRE: 30kr
HAPPY HOURS 22-24
ONKEL DANNYSPLADS 13

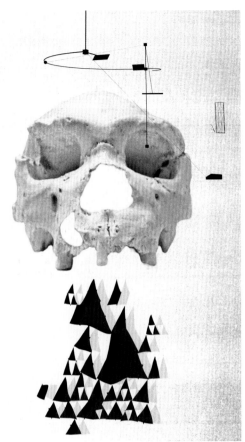

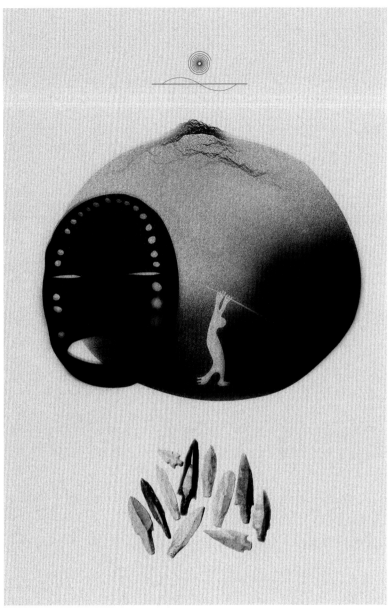

To be launched in 2012

[Top of the opposite page]

<u>Oni Ayhun</u>

Poster and label design for Berlin based artist Oni Ayhun. Illustrations are based on the theme of life cirde. When the record spins, an optical illusion occurs, in which the segments appear to be closed concentric circles.

-

<u>Client</u>
Oni Ayhun

2009

[Bottom of the opposite page]

<u>This Ain´t Havana</u>

Poster and logo design for Copenhagen based club This Ain´t Havana.

-

<u>Client</u>
This Ain´t Havana

2010

[Top] <u>Evolution Posters</u>

Two Posters made on the theme of evolution.

-

<u>Client</u>
Self-initiated

2011

[Bottom] <u>Happy Feet</u>

Here and Away and Red Cross Scandinavia released a painting book for kids and adults to raise money for the Red Cross activities. I contributed "Happy Feet," an illustration based on reflexology and the well being of our body.

-

<u>Client</u>
Here and Away / Red Cross

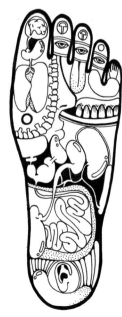

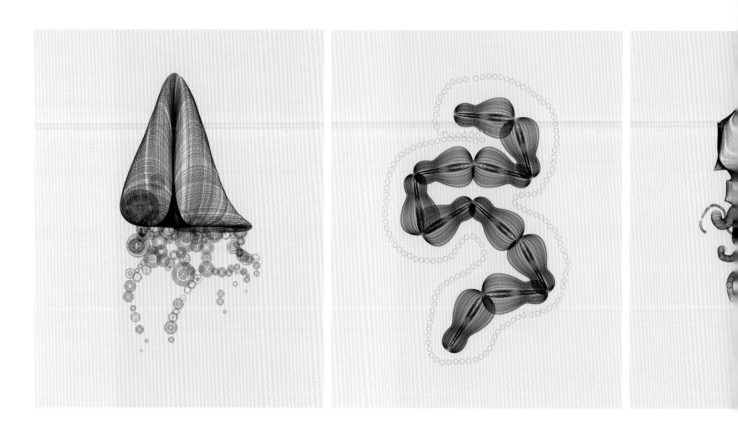

2009

[Above] <u>Aevum incompertus</u>

2009 was Darwin's 200th birthday anniversary. Working with this theme, I created "Aevum incompertus", a bundle of illustrations displaying life forms that are still to be revealed. This project is presented as a poster and in a magazine.
-
<u>Client</u>
Self-initiated

2009

[Right] <u>When Time Falls off the Walls</u>

A screening of an animated piece combined with a live performance by Fredrik Auster in Beijing, China.
-
<u>Client</u>
Self-initiated installation

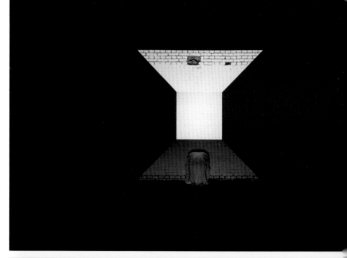

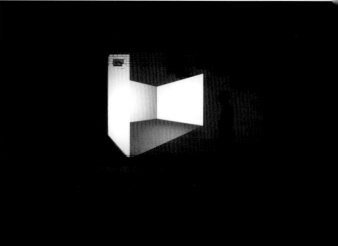

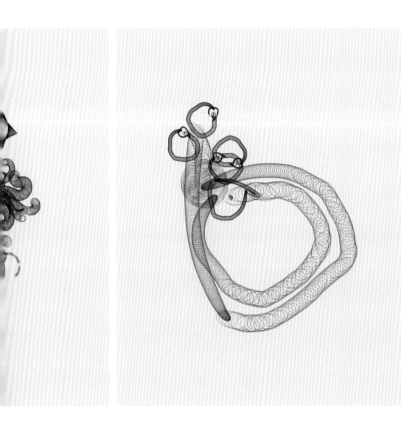

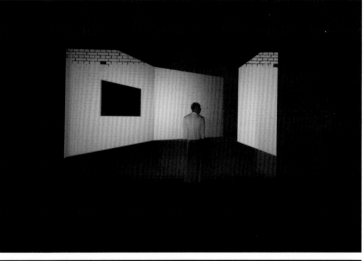

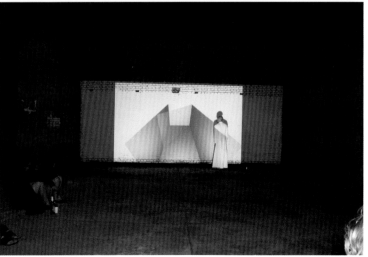

OH YEAH STUDIO
Norway

〜

Oh Yeah Studio is a duo, Christina Magnussen and Hans Christian Øren. They are in their second year of establishment. They met in school where they started collaborating and doing their own "thing". They wanted to make idealistic projects and explore new fields and have fun. Their aim is to seduce, inspire and create emotional responses to all visual projects. A design solution should of course also be innovative and communicative. Today they work widely within the design disciplines. Their services range from illustration, web design, editorial design, packaging design, and brand identity to art direction. In addition they also work with personal projects, such as exhibitions, graphical art prints, posters and murals.

OH YEAH STUDIO 2010

2010
[Above] Oh Yeah Studio

Stick Magazine is an Irish magazine run by students at Limerick Art School. They feature different designers each publication and interviewed us for the March 2010 edition. We made a special Oh Yeah Studio poster and a skateboard deck just for that edition. The illustration is hand drawn abstract objects. It was kind of a tribute to the Great Russian artist El Lizitsky, with a modern touch.

-
Client
Self-initiated

2010
[Right] HI-FI klubben

HI-FI klubben is the biggest chain in Scandinavia with high quality sound and image products like stereos, TVs, loud speakers etc. Rå Lyd is their magazine that targets customers with not only products but more of an experience of good music like concerts and such. This publication's theme was the wonderful musician Jarle Bernhoft. Oh Yeah Studio was hired by Gazette to illustrate the magazine's interior pages. Project in collaboration with Gazette design agency.

OH YEAH STUDIO

2009

Sirens and Us

Siren and Us have deep roots in early progressive rock avant-garde and minimalist contemporary music. The band now meets a more approachable genre in alternative rock. This mixture of genres results in a brand new honest sound with an overall dark and mystical feel.

We focused on the darkness and visualized an obscure and enigmatic world for the viewer to dive into when listening to this wonderful music.
-

Design
Hans Christian Oren when working at Norwegian Ink. In collaboration with Frode Nordbø.

2011

[Bottom] Design vs. Music Poster

We were invited to talk at this year's Design vs Music. This is an annual design event in Tromsø, created by Tank design and Grafill. We also designed the event poster. We built a concept around the word vs. (versus) which is often used in boxing fights and such. It's Design vs. Music and I'm not sure who's winning. For the type treatment we brought in vs. number two. We really wanted to make a naive and rough contrast to the drawn subject where the technique is very realistic and detailed. The effect on the type is fluorescent color+reflex on top, so it will light up nicely in the dark north / Tromsø.

_2008_

[Above] <u>Beautiful/Decay</u>

Beautiful/Decay is the definitive art and design publication showcasing emerging and established contemporary artists. The magazine acts as a go-to, first exposure sourcebook that reveals today's most influential and innovative talents from the creative world. Oh Yeah Studio was contacted to be interviewed for the issue No.X, 2008. In addition to the interview we made an illustration as homage to the good people at B/D.

_2010_

[Right] <u>Silent Shapes</u>

We regularly involve ourselves in art projects to explore new and interesting fields within art and design. This is a personal project called Silent Shapes. The name was set to emphasize the idea we set out to explore. The elements are abstract, organic shapes set in a surreal setting. The project resulted in an exhibition.

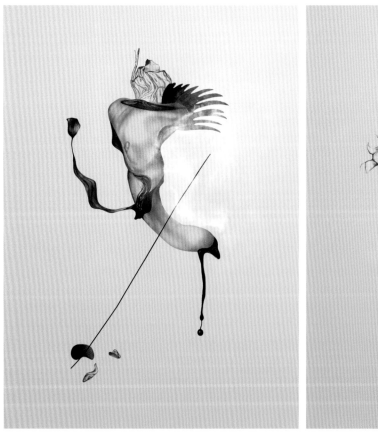

2009

T-shirts for Ministry of Press

Ministry of Press collaborates with designers around the world to bring out high quality t-shirt prints with limited editions. They strive to be unique with original designs based on each designer's distinctive style. Oh Yeah Studio was commissioned to design a series for the March 2009 collection. We based the images on a surreal idea and feeling, combining drawings and abstract shapes to create that street wear look.

She Runs Like an Animal in the Sky

Self-initiated illustration project.

2008

[Top] <u>Whaleless</u>

Pollution and unacceptable fishing practices are seriously endangering the survival of the giant marine mammals. Whaleless is a project dedicated to anyone wishing to express their indignation, rage, shame, disbelief or concern in an arty way. Whaleless is an idea of Giovanni Cervi and Res Pira and is powered by the Italian Pig magazine.
Oh Yeah Studio was excited to contribute to this project which aims to raise money for Greenpeace. The image is an abstract representation of the world under water, the home of the whales. The image was also shown in Computer Arts and has been bought as a picture.

2009

[Bottom] <u>Computer Arts</u>

Computer Arts is a leading design magazine, always up to date on the design arena. Oh Yeah Studio was contacted to design the article "Be more creative", for both the UK and Polish publication. The task was simple, just illustrate something really creative! We built the typography from many different elements to give a complex expression. The "thinking man" was added to emphasize the creative process.

2009-2010

BAR Magazine

BAR is a Norwegian magazine that targets bartenders, waiters in wine bars and pub employees. BAR is also distributed to members of the Norwegian Sommelier Association.

The design and layout aims to bring forward an illustrative expression and make the publication a vivid and playful magazine that changes its appearance from issue to issue.

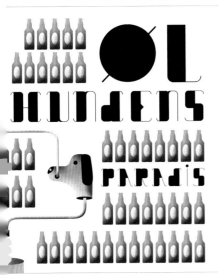

BLEED

Norway

Bleed is a multi-disciplinary design consultancy based in Oslo, Norway, established in June 2000. They work to challenge today's conventions around art, visual language, media and identity.
Bleed's work spans brand identity and development, art direction, packaging, printed matter, interactive design, art projects and exhibitions.
Both their client list and creative output has become diverse and impressive, and made them one of the most awarded agencies in Norway, with international and national acclaim.
They believe in the power of visual language. Their works deals with long term brand-strategies as well as keeping them fresh by constantly challenging the boundaries of design and media.
Bleed for the revolution™.

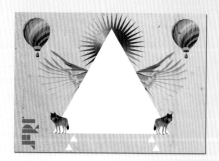

2010
FRI Antismoking program

Posters and flyers for FRI, meaning free in
Norwegian. An Anti-tobacco campaign
for schoolchildren aged from 13-15. The
overall theme is about kids being free to
make their own decisions and not succumb
to peer pressure, and various designs of
talking and thinking capsules work as
graphic tools.
To counter-balance the seriousness of the
message, the visual language is playful
and humorous with naive and quirky photo
collages to make it easier for the kids to
relate to.
-
<u>Client</u>
Norwegian Helsedirektoratet
<u>Design & Illustration</u>
Miriam Skovholt Mortensen

2010

MySpace

MySpace is a shared experience around
global culture that gives curators, tastemakers
and consumers the tools to discover, publish,
and connect based on common interests.
The revitalized brand is fresh, designed as
a vessel that leverages MySpace brand
equity and core culture allowing it to mature
into the most satisfying and engaging social
entertainment entity.
Visually mixing interests and personalities of
the users to give the brand experience room to
grow, we use simple typography and the logo
for different corporate illustrations.
The strong type and material is the base, the
visuals can be random from users of MySpace
or generated by professionals.
-
Client
MySpace Inc
Creative Director
Svein Haakon Lia
Design & Illustration
Svein Haakon Lia, Astrid Feldner

Eve Brooklyn
Creative director

310.869.5010
ebrooklyn@myspace-inc.com
myspace.com

T 310.969.7327 / F 310.969.5010
407 North Maple Drive, 2nd Floor Beverly Hills, CA 90210

407 North Maple Drive, 2nd Floor
Beverly Hills, CA 90210

Brooklyn
creative director

310.869.5010
brooklyn@myspace-inc.com
myspace.com

T +1 310.969.7856 / F +1 310.969.7388
myspace.com

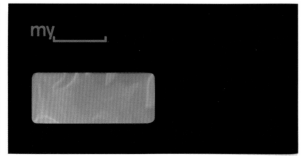
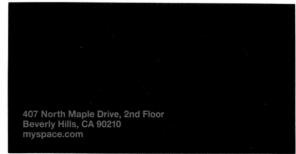

407 North Maple Drive, 2nd Floor
Beverly Hills, CA 90210
myspace.com

Everardo Elizalde
Account Executive
Latin America

Tel +1 310 392 7664
Fax +1 310 392 5661
everardo.elizalde@alu.com

Leave your mark/signature
ALU Inc.
138 West 25th Street
NY 10001
New York, USA
www.alu.com

Robert Rosean
President

Tel +1 201 617 2018
Fax +1 201 617 2044
Cell +1 732 673 9031
robert.rosean@alu.com

Leave your mark/signature
ALU Inc.
138 West 25th Street
NY 10001
New York, USA
www.alu.com

2007

Alu "Leave your mark"

The "leave your mark" concept for ALU 2007 is street art meeting high end fashion. Stencil art and handwriting on top of real life renderings make this something special. We had a fantastic photo shoot and we roughed it up to become a sexy mix of photography and illustration.

-

Client
Alu Italy
Creative Director
Dag Stian Solhaug-Laska
Design & Illustration
Dag Stian Solhaug-Laska, Erik Hedberg

2010

Hunger

Hunger is a word that defines Bleed well. In their 10 years of existence, much has changed in the design world. The studio's spirit, however, is a constant. They are restless, intuitive, and contemplative. They defiantly question convention and the very definition of graphic design. And although they are always thinking – more importantly, they are always doing. Their output is astonishing both in quantity and quality.

Organic and fluid, Bleed is perfectly suited for mutable times. Their culture and environment encourage a strong relationship with nature. This seems to somehow inform their dynamic range and give them an unparalleled flexibility. While many designers appear to feel weighed down by tradition, Bleed never does. With eyes firmly set on the horizon, they continue to blur design, art, and technology to create a visual language that is distinctly Bleed.

-

Client
Bleed
Creative Director
Dag Stian Solhaug-Laska
Design
Bleed

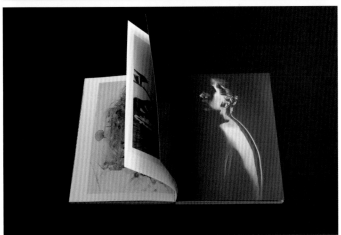

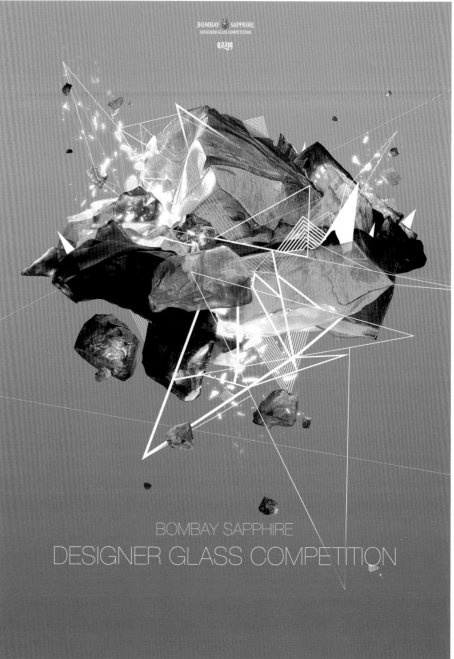

BOMBAY SAPPHIRE
DESIGNER GLASS COMPETITION

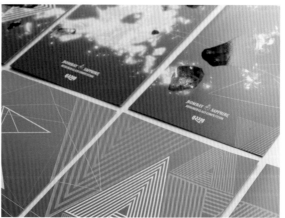

1.

GLOBE
EIVIND NARUM

Glasset er fint i
proporsjonene - klokken
har en klassisk cocktail-
form. Den massive stetten
med et blått parti skaper
tyngde og er et
spennende element.

2.

TORNADO
KRISTIAN ENGLUND &
CASTELNANO SIMOONS

Glasset har en morsom
form, tøft og lekkert på en
gang. Designet har mye
energi og lever godt opp til
sitt navn.

2.

CLEAR CUT
RUDI WULFF

Glasset har en vakker og
klassisk form med en
spennende kombinasjon av
glass og tre, i tillegg er det
både funksjonelt og ivaretar
Bombays eleganse.

2008

**Bombay Sapphire Student Glass
Competition**

Bleed created posters, fliers, and a
website for the prestigious Bombay
Sapphire Designer Glass Competition. The
challenge, aimed primarily at students,
is to create a new, innovative design for
the classic Martini glass. The winner will
represent Norway in the international
finals.

-
Client
Bacardi
Art Director
Astrid Feldner
Design & Illustration
Sebastian Esche

KOKORO & MOI
Finland

•••••••••••

Kokoro & Moi is a multidisciplinary design consultancy specializing in brand identity and development, creative direction, visual communication and interaction. Their clientele represents commercial players from multinationals to start-ups, as well as various cultural and public institutions, who are searching for better concepts and ideas for the future.

They work on a broad range of assignments, from development of brand identity systems or new service concepts to orchestration of complex design projects for print, screen, products and environments. They love asking questions, challenging accepted explanations and inferring possible new worlds.

Kokoro & Moi was founded in 2001 by designers Teemu Suviala and Antti Hinkula.

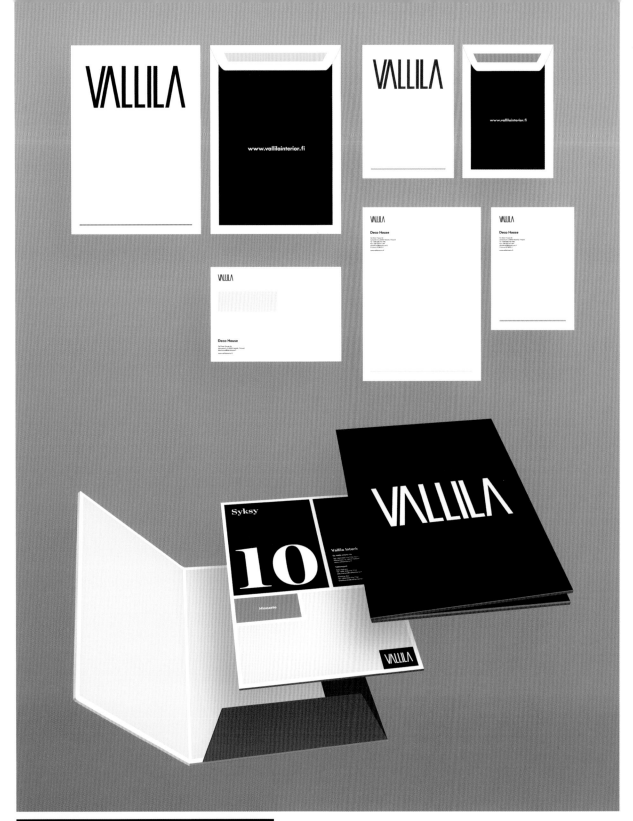

2008

Vallila Interior

Established in 1935, Vallila is a group of companies in the field of interior design and decoration. In 2008 Vallila wanted to refresh the graphic identity of the group with a new unified look for all its subsidiaries in order to ease the future merge of the companies. Kokoro & Moi worked on the brand development project and created one consistent identity for Vallila and helped to refresh the retail image in stores and online.

-

Client
Villila

2009

PLAYFUL – New Finnish Design

PLAYFUL – New Finnish Design was an exhibition
that presented fresh concepts from individual
designers and design companies during the
Meatpacking District Design event held in New York
in May 2009. The focus of the event was on play
and creativity as elementary forces in human life.
Kokoro & Moi is responsible for the PLAYFUL identity
as well as the art direction of all promotional
material from exhibition graphics to the website.

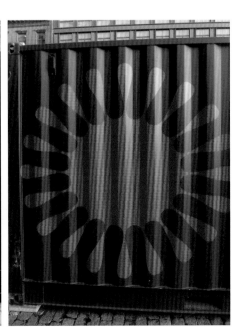

2008
Escalator Records

Escalator Records is a Japanese record label, a record store and a café in Shibuya, Tokyo. The label hosts artists such as Yukari Fresh, Miniflex and Avalon.
Kokoro & Moi has designed the identity for the record label and the Escalator Café, graphics and music packaging for two compilation series, We Are Escalator Records and We Were Escalator Records, as well as prints for Escalator Records clothing.

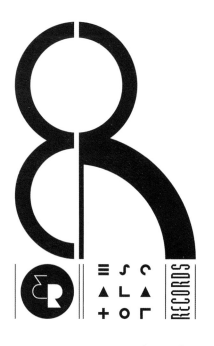

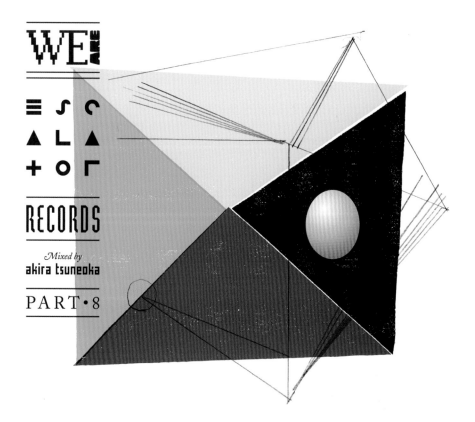

WORLD
DESIGN
CAPITAL

HELSINKI
2012

WORLD
DESIGN
CAPITAL
HELSINKI
2012

WWW.WDCHELSINKI2012.FI

WORLD DESIGN CAPITAL HELSINKI 2012 IS THE
GLOBAL ROLE MODEL IN USING DESIGN AS THE KEY
DRIVER IN REINVENTING THE CITY.

FOR US, DESIGN IS ABOUT FINDING SOLUTIONS TO
CITIZENS' NEEDS THROUGH INNOVATIVE DESIGN
AND USER-DRIVEN PERSPECTIVES.

WORLD DESIGN CAPITAL HELSINKI 2012 HAS A
STRONG DESIGN TRADITION, A RAPIDLY CHANGING
URBAN STRUCTURE, AND A SHARED VISION TO
BECOME A GLOBAL LEADER WHERE DESIGN IS THE
CATALYST FOR A BETTER SOCIETY.

WORLD DESIGN CAPITAL HELSINKI 2012 IS THE
GLOBAL ROLE MODEL IN USING DESIGN AS THE KEY
DRIVER IN REINVENTING THE CITY.

FOR US, DESIGN IS ABOUT FINDING SOLUTIONS TO
CITIZENS' NEEDS THROUGH INNOVATIVE DESIGN
AND USER-DRIVEN PERSPECTIVES.

WORLD DESIGN CAPITAL HELSINKI 2012 HAS A
STRONG DESIGN TRADITION, A RAPIDLY CHANGING
URBAN STRUCTURE, AND A SHARED VISION TO
BECOME A GLOBAL LEADER WHERE DESIGN IS THE
CATALYST FOR A BETTER SOCIETY.

2011
[Left] <u>World Design Capital Helsinki 2012</u>

In the beginning of 2009, Kokoro & Moi was
chosen to design The World Design Capital 2012
application for the city of Helsinki, taking their home
city to the finals together with the city of Eindhoven, in
competition with 46 other cities.
After successful work in the application phase,
Kokoro & Moi is continuing the project with the city
of Helsinki and developing an open identity concept
and communication design for the year 2012.

2010
[Bottom] <u>Lahti Biennale</u>

Established in 2009, Lahti Biennale is a major design
event series taking place in the city of Lahti, Finland,
biennially. Incorporating renowned events such as
the Olo.Muoto fair and the Lahti International Poster
Biennial, it will play an important role in showcasing
new thinking and design during the World Design
Capital year 2012.
Kokoro & Moi is responsible for the visual identity,
art direction and design of posters, books and other
promotional campaign materials for Lahti Biennale.

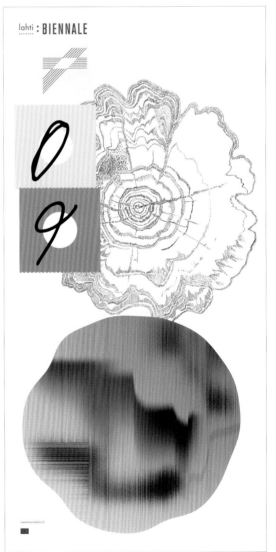

lahti : BIENNALE

JANINE REWELL
Finland
••••••••••

Janine Rewell is a Helsinki-based illustrator and graphic designer. She studied at the University of Art and Design Helsinki and Rhode Island School of Design. Janine won a bronze Design Lion at the Cannes Lions International Advertising Festival 2009 and was nominated by Print Magazine as one of the Twenty Best New Visual Artists of 2010. She was also awarded with the Junior Award in 2010, a great national recognition for a young designer. In addition to taking part in many group exhibitions, she has had solo exhibitions in Barcelona and Poland. Inspired by the geometry of nature, decorative details and intense colors, Janine's designs are an enchanting mix of Scandinavian design and Slavic folk art.

2011
[Left] <u>Brummel</u>
Magazine Cover Illustration.
-
<u>Client</u>
Brummel Magazine
<u>Illustration</u>
Janine Rewell

2011
<u>Finnair</u>
Campaign illustrations for a Finnish Airline. The three animals illustrate three continents: USA, Europe and Asia.
-
<u>Client</u>
Finnair
<u>Creative Direction</u>
Advertising Agency SEK & Grey
<u>Illustration</u>
Janine Rewell

2011
[Left] <u>Birth of the Swan</u>

A print made for a touring Finnish illustration exhibition.
-
<u>Client</u>
Finnish Cultural Institute for the Benelux & Agent Pekka
<u>Illustration</u>
Janine Rewell

2011
[Bottom] <u>Flesh Flutes</u>

Promotional poster made for my solo exhibition in Poland.
-
<u>Client</u>
Gallery Fundacja SPOT.
<u>Design & Illustration</u>
Janine Rewell

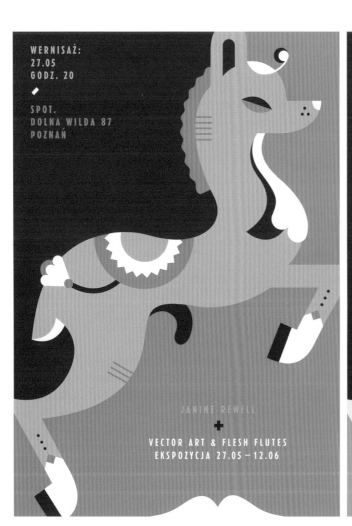

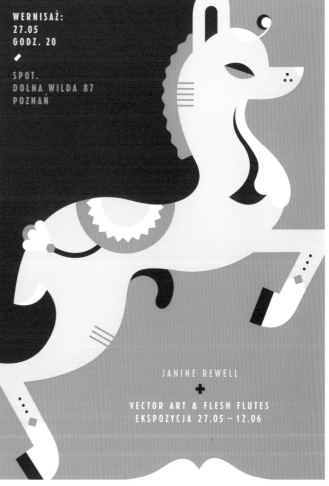

2009-2010

Nokia Christmas

An illustration work created for Nokia's Christmas campaign in the UK in 2009-2010. The illustrations functioned as the main element throughout the campaign. The illustrations were mainly seen in print advertising; billboards, magazines and 6sheets, but were also used in Nokia's store, packaging, and online presence.

Client
Nokia
Creative Direction
Wieden & Kennedy London
Illustration
Janine Rewell
Copywriter
Wieden & Kennedy London

SIGGI ODDS

Iceland

Sigurður Oddsson, Siggi Odds for short, was born in
Reykjavík, Iceland in 1985, but spent a large part of
his childhood in Vancouver, Canada. He graduated
with a B.A. degree in Graphic Design/Communication
Arts from the Iceland Academy of the Arts, Reykjavík,
Iceland in the spring of 2008.
He enjoys design, type and illustration, working
primarily with people in the music, fashion and arts
industries as well as making identities for businesses
people whose vision he can relate to. Although he
has done work in various styles, he'd like to think this
collection of work can be seen as some sort of whole,
showcasing his general approach to design.

[Right] <u>Þórarinn Eldjárn</u>

This book cover was made for Þórarinn Eldjárn, one
of Iceland's most prominent authors. It is a collection
of poetry about various aspects of life, with words of
wisdom, short eccentric poems and more.
I chose to represent the broad spectrum of the contents
in colorful ribbons falling and twirling from the sky.

[Bottom] <u>Arte Creative Wallpaper</u>

I was asked to create an artist's wallpaper
background for the launch of Arte Creative's new
website. I made an accidentally erotic composition of
logs and sheets falling in an undefined space. I also
started to see faces in the shading of the sheets and
then emphasized them from then on.

ÞÓRARINN ELDJÁRN
VÍSNAFÝSN

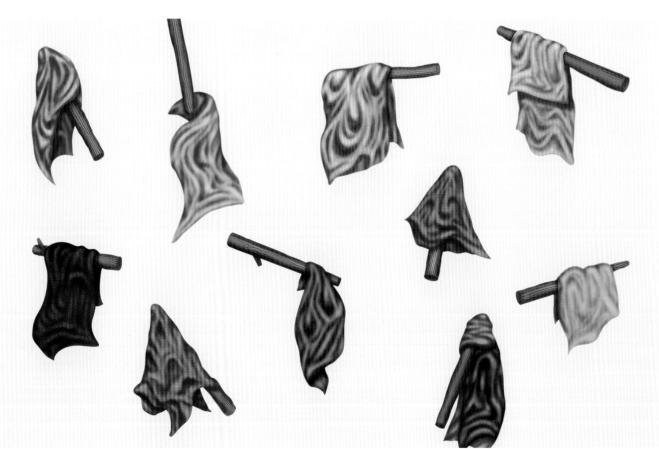

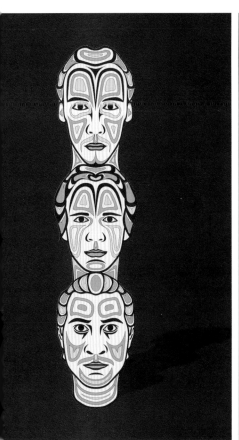

[Top left] <u>Totem</u>

I made this totem illustration of two of my friends and myself to promote our birthday potlatch, which sadly never happened.

[Top right] <u>Mesópótamía</u>

Cover art for Mesópótamía by Icelandic band Sykur.

<u>Lundi & Metaface</u>

These are a couple of illustrations I made as tests while I was working on my graduation exhibition. They are illustrations in the style of my take on Northwest Coast native art, or how I understood it at the time. I am still quite happy with these two, as they came early in my progression in the style and, as tests, perhaps have more of me in them than the triptych in my exhibition. I am still working on developing my own take on this style.

Sequences

Sequences is a real-time art festival in Reykjavík, Iceland hosted annually by The Living Arts Museum. They approached Jónas Valtýsson, Sveinn Davíðsson and me for the design and art direction of the festival. We teamed up, with Mundi helping for some parts, and produced printed material and a website for this ever-growing festival.
The final product consists of an idea of milk captured in time, hinting at the festival's real-time focus – with strong typography overlaying the b/w image with a screaming bright color. The posters and printed material were printed in two color offset, black and a bright PMS 805 by an environmental friendly printer.

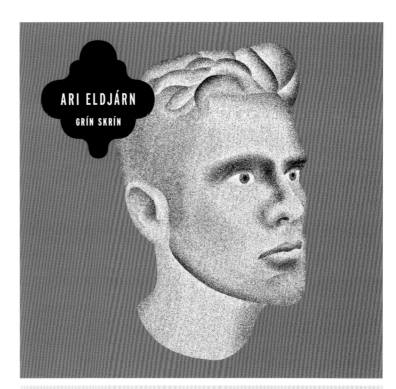

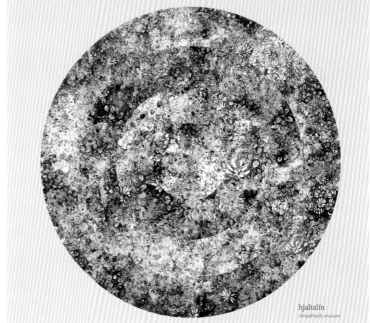

Ari Eldjárn

Ari Eldjárn is from a line of great Icelandic gentlemen. His grandfather was Kristján Eldjárn, one time president of Iceland and his father is Þórarinn Eldjárn, renowned author and poet.
He asked me to do the cover and I rendered his face to appear somewhere between a Roman statue and a 1930s airbrushed cover illustration. I decided to use only the color black and one of my favorite colors, PMS 805 neon orange/red/pink. The disc was folded into a four-fold, one-piece cover with clever cuts to hold it in place.

Sleepdrunk Seasons - Hjaltalín

For this project, the band Hjaltalín approached me with an idea to design the cover for their debut album, Sleepdrunk Seasons, using artwork of the renowned Icelandic floral painter Eggert Pétursson. I used only one painting for the entire album artwork, applying the painter's great span of scale – going from the large picture to the detail, the vastness of the color to the single flower using a predetermined process of manual scaling.

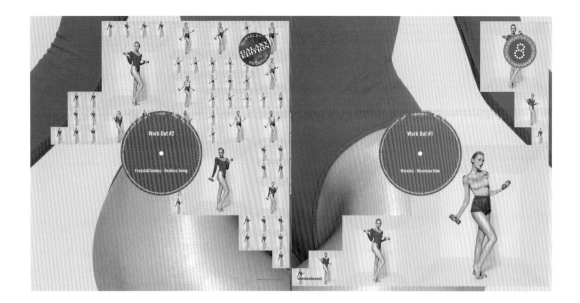

2009

Wareika/Fredski&Tomboy - Work Out #1

An experience in catching balls, thrown into the air by label boss Fredski from Tartelet, who wished for a photographic cover with a fitness theme for this mixed artist EP. The brief took me out of my regular waters conceptually, which is a really good idea from time to time.

<u>Client</u>
Tartelet Records
<u>Design</u>
Christian Zander
<u>Photography</u>
Nikolaj Holm Møller
<u>Hair&Make up</u>
Lasse Pedersen
<u>Stylist</u>
Sebastián Machado
<u>Model</u>
Amalie Lind

THE EMPEROR OF ANTARCTICA

Denmark

▬▬▬▬▬▬▬▬

Blurring the boundaries between the ambiguity of fine art and the modern aestheticism of graphic design, Bucharest-based Dane, The Emperor of Antarctica (*1983), works in multiple disciplines but communicates his interests and obsessions coherently and consistently across a range of creative platforms.
Taking on the twin roles of graphic designer and artist, the versatile creative produces visual art that is perhaps best described as neutral yet intricate meditations on form and human perception. The large-scale laser prints inspired by mathematics, symmetrical, Islamic construction patterns, and his developing interest in introspectively, subvert the traditional distinction between form and content by seeking a purity of form that is inherently suspicious of narrative intent. In this way, the Emperor of Antarctica can be seen as an exponent of a complex dynamic that forces the viewer to contemplate the significance of form without narrative, matter without story.

2011

<u>Mikkel Metal - Cassini/Mazurski</u>

Yet another variation on my pattern work, this one explores the boundaries between order and chaos by combining open and closed tilings in one system. The b-side pushes the point further by employing a two color print to prove the Four Color Theorem.

-
<u>Client</u>
Tartelet Records
<u>Design</u>
Christian Zander

2011

<u>Samuel André Madsen - Love like this</u>
<u>EP</u>

Another variation on my pattern work, a fully open ended and dynamic version of the same tiling system used for Mikkel Metal and my work for Brandt Brauer Frick (not shown). A drug fueled moment of pure inspiration accounts for the addition of the cartoon faces; some might say it's a reflection of the sample-laden filter house found on the vinyl.

-
<u>Client</u>
Tartelet Records
<u>Design</u>
Christian Zander

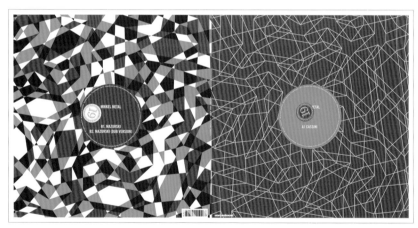

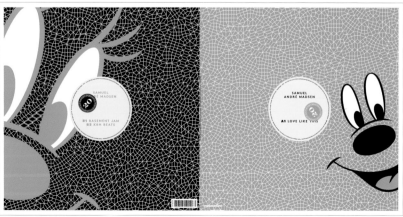

2009

[Left] My Body, My Business

A poster made for the backside of the festival's newspaper. It features a selection of items with little obvious connections. The pattern/ composition is a rational system that folds on itself and could go on forever expanding like this. It included the photo of Apollo 17 returning back to earth from outer space, my own silhouette with stars bursting, of course all point to the trials and joys of drug induced dancing at a techno festival.

-
Client
Distortion Festival
Design
Christian Zander
Photography
NASA

2009

[Bottom]

Wareika - Ascending/Descending

The direction for this came from the organic sound of the band, which inspires me to move outside my regular, mostly flat and graphic approach and into a full on raster mode. I wanted to explore a painting like the process of layering "strokes" to create images that are hard to define as anything other than organic texture.

-
Client
Tartelet Records
Design
Christian Zander
Photography
Landsat 7

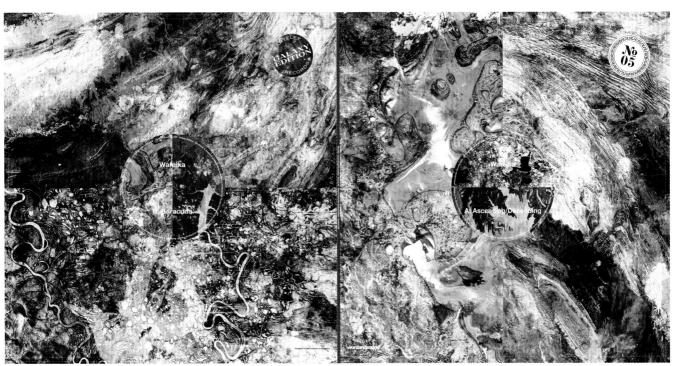

THE EMPEROR OF ANTARCTICA

2009

I Got You On Tape - Spinning for the Cause

The cover for the award winning Best Danish Album of 2009 is a simple exploration of the meaning of layers (are there 2 or 3?), and of the rotation of a square.

Client
Tigerspring
Design
Christian Zander
Photography
NASA

2009

[Opposite page]

moi Caprice - All We Fear is Love

The assignment to design moi Caprice's greatest hits compilation came shortly after the I.G.Y.O.T. cover, as the bands knew each other well. I tried for 3 weeks to paint the intro to M.A.S.H. but it didn't turn out the way I wanted. The day before I had to submit the artwork, I woke up with the idea of amalgamating my striped bed sheets, Gorsky's Russian turn of the century photos, my own 10 year old snapshots and acrylic paint. Again it turned out to be a further exploration of the concept of layering.

Client
Glorious Records
Design
Christian Zander
Photography
Christian Zander & Sergey Mikhaylovich Prokudin-Gorsky

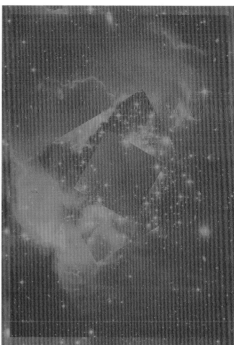

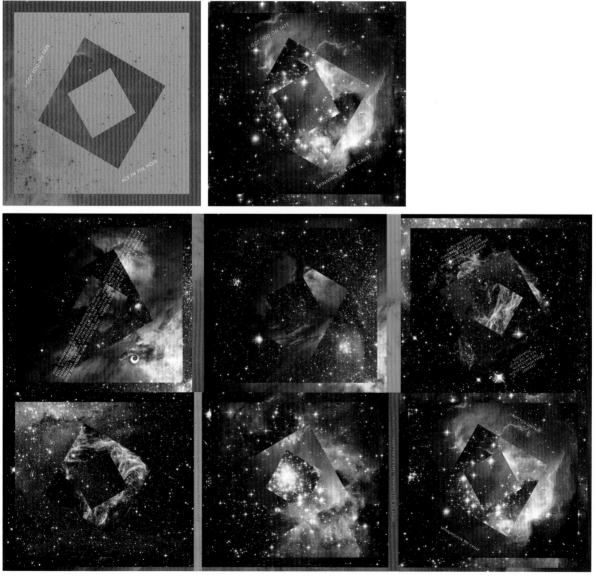

Thank you so much everyone who helped us through the years. A special thanks to Christian and Ulrich for some glorious years.

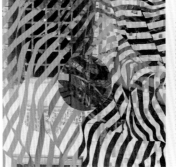

THE EMPEROR OF ANTARCTICA

HVASS&HANNIBAL
Denmark

︿︿︿︿︿︿︿︿︿︿

Hvass&Hannibal is a multi-disciplinary arts and design studio based in Copenhagen. Since 2006, its founders Nan Na Hvass & Sofie Hannibal have worked in close collaborative partnership with illustrative and conceptual design in a number of different fields for numerous clients in Europe, Asia and the US. Whether in the digital realm or on a three-dimensional scale, the studio takes projects from esoteric illustrative beginnings to a full art direction and graphic design solution, all in-house. As well as being image makers they have also directed high profile photographic projects, and created sets and costumes for, among others, one of Denmark's famous musical successes of recent years - Efterklang.

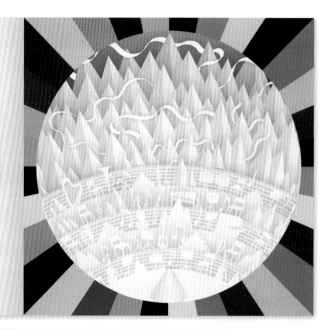

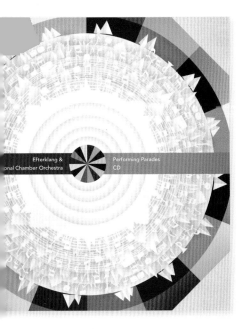

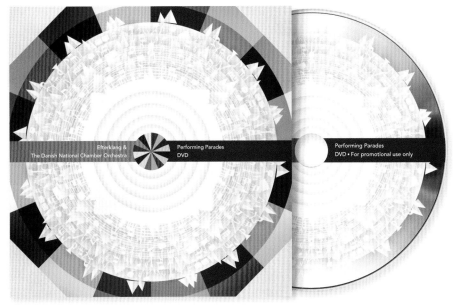

2009

Efterklang – Performing Parades

In the autumn of 2008 the Danish band
Efterklang performed their entire album
Parades with the Danish National Chamber
Orchestra at DR in Copenhagen. Apart from
creating the stage design and costumes for
the actual concert, we have also designed
the packaging for the album and DVD. In
our design we have tried to incorporate the
different elements that we used in the actual
set design and the costumes.

-
Client
Efterklang, Rumraket and the Leaf Label

2009

[Right] Efterklang – Magic Chairs

Album cover artwork for Efterklang's third full
length album Magic Chairs.
We did the design and art direction, and
once again photographer Brian Buchard
helped us with the photo for the actual album
cover, which is taken at Thorvaldsens Museum
in Copenhagen.

-
Client
Efterklang, Rumraket and 4AD
Photography
Brian Buchard

2009

Hvass&Hannibal at Allmänna Galleriet

In 2009 we put up a show at Allmänna
Galleriet in Stockholm. In continuation of
our exhibition at MOHS earlier that year we
painted giant murals directly on the walls.
The patterns are inspired by traditional
patchwork techniques and images used for
meditation.

Client
Allmänna Galleriet
Project Assistants
Linn Wie, Lasse Gyrn

Hvass&Hannibal på Allmänna Galleriet

Kronobergsgatan 37 · Stockholm · 8. september - 17. oktober

2010

<u>Clogs – The Creatures in the Garden of</u>
<u>Lady Walton</u>

Album cover artwork for Clogs' EP Veil Waltz
(left) and their 5th album, The Creatures in the
Garden of Lady Walton.
The album includes a collection of new songs
composed by Padma Newsome during his
2005 residency at Giardini La Mortella, a rich
botanical paradise created by Lady Walton on
the island of Ischia, off the Bay of Naples in
Italy. Our imagery is an attempt at visualizing
how we imagine the garden, in accordance to
the music. Many of the creatures and plants in
the imagery are taken from Padma's lyrics.

<u>Client</u>
Clogs / Brassland

2007

[Right] Turboweekend – After Hours

Single cover for Turboweekend, After Hours.

<u>Client</u>
Turboweekend / Copenhagen Records

0000

Turboweekend - Ghost of a Chance

Turboweekend released their second album on March 23rd 2009, and as usual we have designed the album cover. The setting is in the mystery of a forest after dark. We folded a magic ball out of paper and took it into the woods together with the photographer Brian Buchard, who has helped us once again with his amazing skills.
-
<u>Client</u>
Turboweekend / Mermaid Records
<u>Photography</u>
Brian Buchard

2007

Turboweekend - Nightshift

We created a visual identity for the Copenhagen based
electronic rock trio. This included designing album covers,
clothes, sets and props that gave the band an all around visual
impact for their audience of fun- and party loving youngsters.
-
Client
Turboweekend / Copenhagen Records
Photography
Brian Buchard

ALL THE WAY TO PARIS

Denmark

ATWTP is a Danish-Swedish graphic design studio based in Copenhagen that was founded in 2004 by Tanja Vibe and Petra Olsson Gendt. They work conceptually with visual communication on both a small and large scale. Elin Kinning joined ATWTP in 2006 and Matilde Rasmussen joined in 2008. They're currently a team of six persons.

2009

Circus Hein

Danish artist Jeppe Hein has curated a circus show at Atelier Calder, Saché, and in FRAC Orleans. 35 artists, designers and architects are participating - ATWTP is among these. We designed the identity, poster, website and exhibition for the show.

-

Client
Jeppe Hein

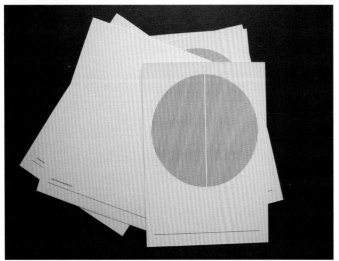

2010
In Praise of Shadows
In Praise of Shadows is a new architecture studio in Stockholm, founded and run by architects Katarina Lundeberg and Fredric Benesch. We love their work and their poetic name and designed a moon composed of straight lines as their identity.

ıu
PRAISE
oɟ
SHADOWS

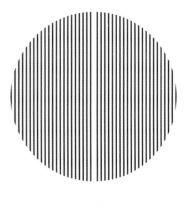

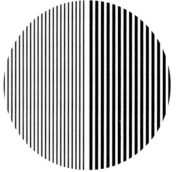

2009

Rebekka Notkin

Copenhagen jeweler Rebekka Notkin just opened her new atelier in Bredgade. The hand drawn emblem is the centerpiece of her new identity. Diamonds are a girl's best friend.

Rebekka
NOTKIN

Bredgade 25
1260 Copenhagen K
+45 33 32 02 60

rebekkanotkin.com

Rebekka
NOTKIN

2010
<u>**Sing Tehus**</u>
New label design for Sing Tehus. The first label is by
ATWTP for the Japanese tea assortment.

Sing
Tehus

Genmaicha
Japanese green tea with roasted rice
玄米茶

www.singtehus.dk

Sing
Tehus

Gyokuro
The finest of Japanese green tea
玉露

www.singtehus.dk

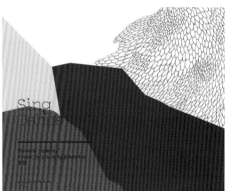

Sing
Tehus

Shincha "new tea"
Finest 1st plucking green tea
新茶

www.singtehus.dk

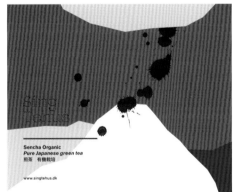

Sing
Tehus

Sencha Organic
Pure Japanese green tea
煎茶　有機栽培

www.singtehus.dk

Sing
Tehus

Hojicha
Roasted gren tea
ほうじ茶

www.singtehus.dk

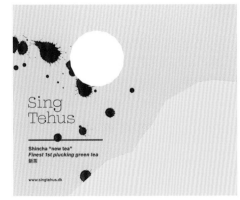

Sing
Tehus

Shincha "new tea"
Finest 1st plucking green tea
新茶

www.singtehus.dk

Sing
Tehus

Sencha
Fresh Japanese green tea
煎茶

www.singtehus.dk

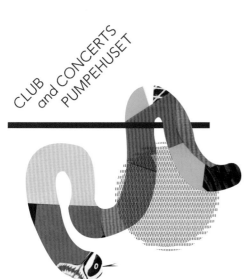

2009

Pumpehuset Rabal Børnekultur

The Rabal-snake, colors and collages
are made for Pumpehuset's children's
stage. This new initiative focuses on
giving the Copenhagen kids a scene
for great music and culture.

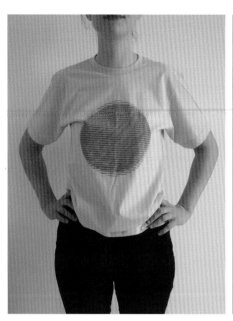

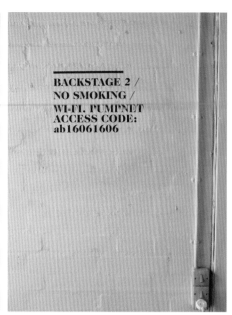

BACKSTAGE 2 /
NO SMOKING /
WI-FI. PUMPNET
ACCESS CODE:
ab16061606

2009

<u>Pumpehuset</u>

Identity for Pumpehuset, a club and concert venue in
Copenhagen.

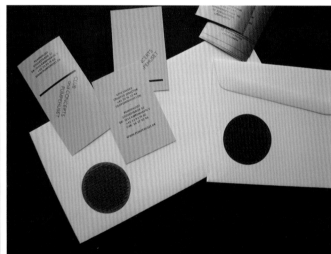

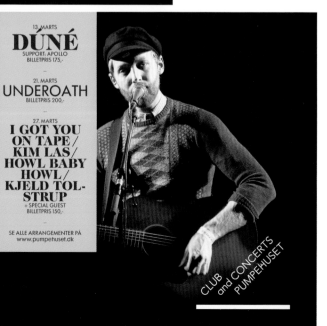

GEIST

2011
<u>**Geist**</u>
Identity for the Restaurant Geist in Copenhagen.

2011

<u>The White Out</u>

The Danish fine carpenters association
made an exhibition with white chairs
made by around 20 Danish designers. The
exhibition started at Ordrupgaard outside
of Copenhagen, travelled on to Tokyo and
is now in London.

38 spritnye, sprithvide stole / 38 nytænkende møbeloverraskelser / 38 fabulerende prototyper skabt af SE medlemmmer og gæsteudstillere

www.se-design.dk

ÅBNINGSTIDER
Tirsdag, torsdag, fredag 13-17. Onsdag 13-19
Weekend og helligdage 11-17
Mandag lukket
www.ordrupgaard.dk

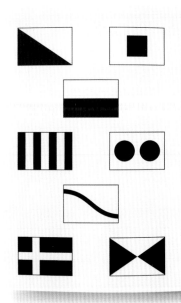

**Momentum,
the North, Moss,
Art and the World**

**Dag Aak Sveinar
Director**

RESEARCH AND DEVELOPMENT
Sweden

◇◇◇◇◇◇◇◇◇◇◇◇◇

Research and Development collaborates with artists, curators, critics, collectors, directors, museums and cultural institutions. They design books, catalogues, posters, exhibition graphics, identity programs and other kinds of printed matter. Occasionally they arrange film screenings and produce or participate in exhibitions.

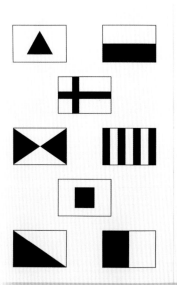

Favoured Nations

**Stina Högkvist
Lina Džuverović**

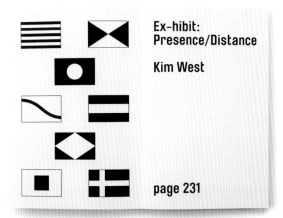

**Ex-hibit:
Presence/Distance**

Kim West

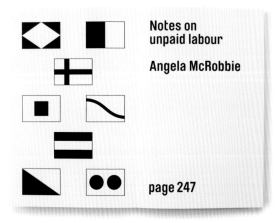

**Notes on
unpaid labour**

Angela McRobbie

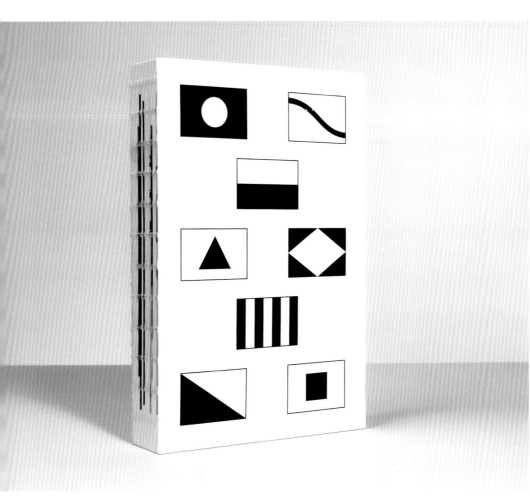

2009

Favoured Nations

Momentum is the biggest art biennial in the Scandinavian region; this year entitled Favored Nations. Participating artists this year are from Denmark, Finland, Iceland, Norway and Sweden. Curated by Stina Högkvist and Lina Dzuverovic.
-
<u>Client</u>
Momentum, the Nordic Biennial of Contemporary Art

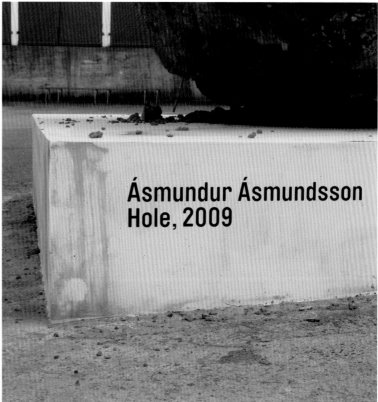

2009

[Above] <u>Favoured Nations</u>

Momentum is the biggest art biennial in the Scandinavian region; this year entitled Favored Nations. Participating artists this year are from Denmark, Finland, Iceland, Norway and Sweden. Curated by Stina Högkvist and Lina Dzuverovic.

-

<u>Client</u>
Momentum, the Nordic Biennial of Contemporary Art

2010

[Right]

<u>Architecture is Made</u>

Identity for Swedish architecture office Architecture is Made.

-

<u>Client</u>
Architecture is Made

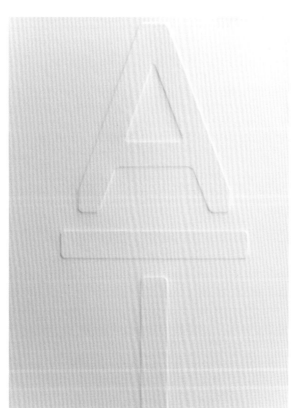

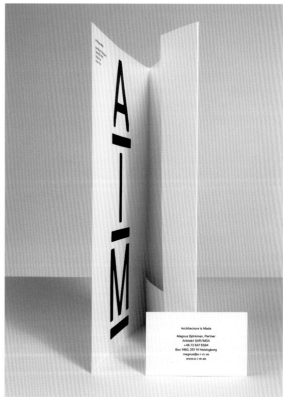

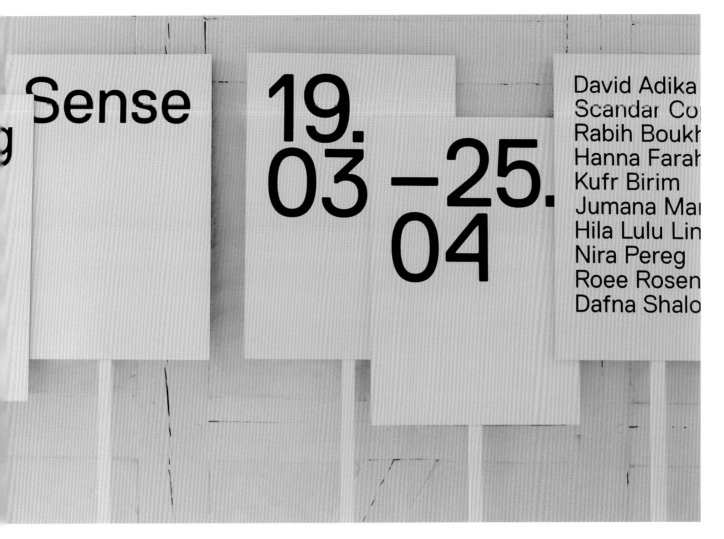

2010
Stop Making Sense
Signage system for the exhibition Stop Making Sense at
Oslo Fine Art Society. Curated by Marianne Hultman.
-
Client
Oslo Fine Art Society

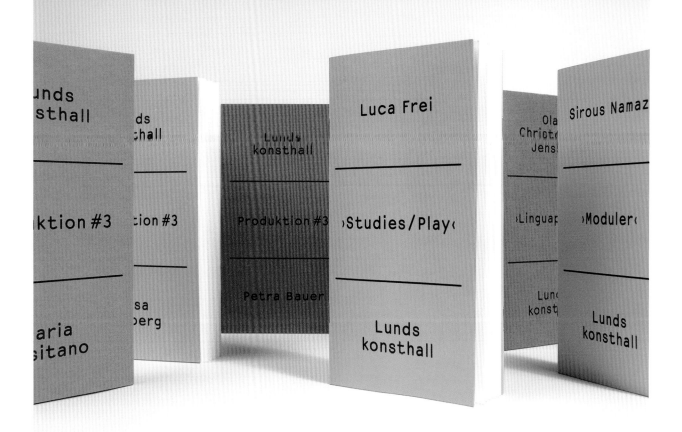

2009

Lunds Konsthall

An exhibition catalogues series presenting different artists' work
for Lunds Konsthall. Since the cover is Z-shaped it enables two
inserts: one for text and the other for images. The catalogues
lack a back page but instead have two front pages.

-
Client
Lunds Konsthall
Photography
Terje Östling

Flávia Müller Medeiros

Unfinished works
Concepts in the sketch book
Unrealised projects
There is something missing works
Works in the drawer
Ongoing failed attempts
Works in need of exhibition
context to complete their meaning
Works in need of commission
Side projects
Ongoing obsessive drawings
Works I've been working on for a
long time but never resolved
Works I always wanted to make
Haruhi Hayashi
Flávia Müller Medeiros
Beltran Obregon

26-29 April 2010

Haruhi Hayashi

Beltran Obregon

2009
Flávia Müller Medeiros

Booklet on the occasion of the Flávia Müller
Medeiros, Haruhi Hayashi and Beltran Obregon
exhibition at R&D studio. Essay by Eugenia Bell,
design editor at Frieze Magazine. Printed on the
R&D Risograph press during the opening. Bound
by the visitors.
-
Client
Flávia Müller Medeiros, Haruhi Hayashi and Beltran
Obregon

FMM: What was your response to the concept of this exhibition project and why did you choose these specific works to develop?

HH: The reason I chose these works was different in each case. The first piece is a series of water-colour drawings of gem stones. I've been working on these for a long time but I never felt satisfied.

BO: The first work I thought about when you mentioned the idea of the exhibition was the work 'Broken Olympus', which consists of a package especially made for a pocket photo camera that I bought years ago and is now broken. A package is basically a container that protects goods from damage during transport, but which also displays information about them and at the same time is designed to attract buyers. [...] I made several versions of this package some years ago but I was not able to resolve certain issues. I suppose the main problem was that the object itself, being a disposable, had a presence or identity that claimed to make it operate differently from the traditional 'art object'. None of the possibilities I envisioned for displaying it convinced me and I felt this work was not quite meant to be just shown as an art work in a gallery context, it just didn't communicate all the things it had to say.

FMM: For a long time I have imagined and kept works in my head convinced that having thought of these works made them finished. [...] avoiding dealing with the fear of transforming thoughts into works as thoughts are always more perfect than when made. One work I'm showing is 'a song that makes you feel like you can do anything', which is a collection of songs I compiled from asking different people, already dealing with expectation, failure and illusion...

HH: [...] the word 'finished' is tricky. I like when the work

looks not so finished and this feeling of openness is important. [...] Sometimes I over-finish work so I have to undo it. When I see artworks I like I feel I'm looking at the 'thinking process'. It is hard to have good balance between thinking and making.

About the artists

Haruhi Hayashi born in Japan, based in London, gained her MA Visual Arts from Goldsmiths College (2004). Recent exhibitions include, 'Auction In A Suitcase', I:I projects, Rome; 'Eau Sauvage part II', Fieldgate Gallery, London; 'Peach', Galerie Eugen Lendl, Graz; 'Time Pop', Prince Charles Cinema, London; 'Revenge of Romance', temporary-contemporary, London.

Flávia Müller Medeiros born in Brazil, based in London, gained her MA Visual Arts from Goldsmiths College (2004). Recent exhibitions include, (solo) 'Failed, Emerging and Young', Stanley Picker Gallery, London; 'Verb: to read and write', Bury St Edmunds, Suffolk; 'The Infinite, The Intimate and The Impossible', Magacin u Kraljevica Marka, Belgrade; 'Showtime', Gasworks, London.

Beltran Obregon Colombian, based in London, gained his MA Visual Arts from Goldsmiths College (2004). Recent exhibitions include, (solo) 'Committee for the Appreciation of Color and Form', Galeria Valenzuela Klenner, Bogota; 'Laid Together on the Lookout', Danielle Arnaud Gallery, London; 'Prison', Bloomberg Space, London; 'Territory of Freedom', Moscow Centre for the Arts, Moscow.

A New York based writer and critic, Eugenia Bell is the design editor of Frieze magazine, where she writes and commissions articles on design and architecture. Her experience in writing and publishing also includes work for

Unfinished works

Concepts in the sketch book

Unrealised projects

There is something missing works

WE RECOMMEND
Denmark

WE RECOMMEND is a multi-disciplinary design agency focusing on visual identity and profile creating design. They help companies, organizations and products to attract attention and be remembered. By translating core values into strong visual concepts, they enable the desired communication with the target group. Their approach to graphic design is based on a Scandinavian simplicity, in which contemporary and strong solutions are rooted in the traditional craftsmanship of graphic design.
WE RECOMMEND was founded in 2004 and is run by designers Martin Fredricson and Nikolaj Knop.

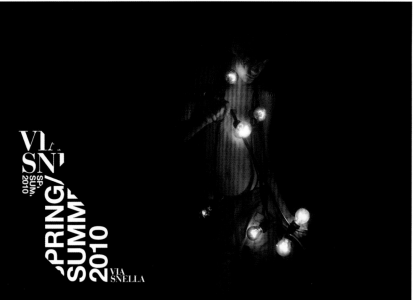

2008

Via Snella Visual Identity

Via Snella is one of the new brands in the prominent Swedish fashion industry. With the ambition for international distribution through a strong brand, Via Snella needed a visual identity that could express its foundation, and at the same time be able to adapt to the looks of the changing seasons within the fashion industry. We met these demands by creating an identity with one foot in classic timelessness and the other in the constantly shifting expressions of modern fashion.

-
Client
Via Snella
Design and Illustration
Martin Fredricson, Nikolaj Knop

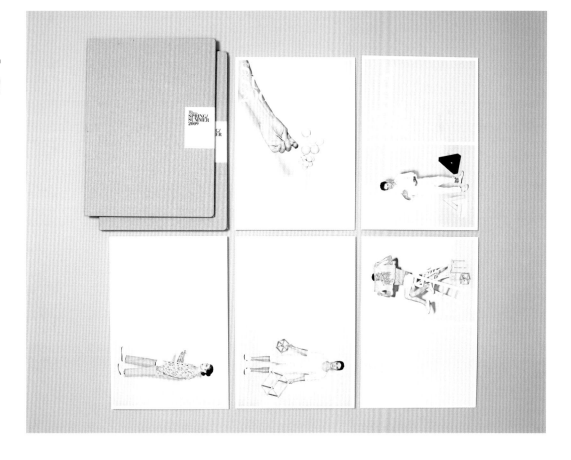

PHILIP BATTIN

Denmark

Philip Battin is a strategic designer, creative entrepreneur and design critic from Denmark. His projects have been acknowledged by internationally acclaimed design publications and organizations and have won numerous awards. In 2009 he was rewarded The Danish Ministry of Culture's Travelling Scholarship and the following year the conference "New Media Days" proclaimed Philip Battin "one of 38 young new media talents to watch". Philip Battin is currently finishing his BA in Design at The Royal Danish Academy of Fine Arts, School of Design.

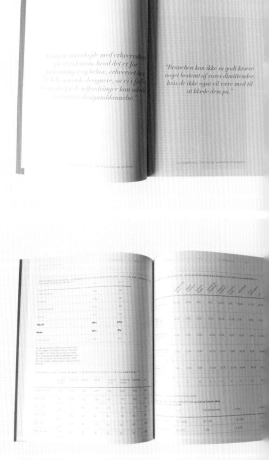

[Opposite page] Redesign Proposal for FILTER

The mission of the photography magazine FILTER is to discuss the effect of photography on our daily lives: on our ways of thinking, of creating history and politics, of constructing a society and undertaking scientific research, of being creative and producing art.
Through in-depth articles, critical commentary, essays, journalism, portraits, reviews and extensive photographic content, FILTER exposes and discusses the innumerable forms and meanings of photography.
-
Client
Self-initiated school assignment

2009

[Bottom] DKDS Publikation

Publication for Danish Fashion Institute, MOKO and Danmarks Designskole concerning the relationship between fashion education and the fashion industry. The layout is inspired by classic book aesthetics set in antique typefaces printed in only pantone light grey and black on Swedish Munken Pure paper.
-
Client
The Danish Design School, Danish Fashion Institute & MOKO
Design
Philip Battin, Ulrik Ejlers

2007

[Above] Josef Muller Bockwurst

Josef Müller-Brockmann influenced me in the way I experience graphic design today. Since he was born in Rapperswil, Switzerland, he must have enjoyed the Swiss Bockwurst – a fat meat sausage. It is often served on a bed of lettuce with onion, tomato, egg & dressing.
By joining together the Swiss bockwurst and the Josef Müller-Brockmann, you cannot avoid ending up with something very beautiful and unique.
The result is this screenprint. The grid is based on the original Zurich Tonhalle Concert Poster, from 1954.

2008

When Saints Go Machine - EP

Visual identity and art direction for up and coming Danish electro-pop group "When Saints Go Machine". The visual direction reflects the futuristic and merging sound. The universe contains dynamism and complexity, as well as minimal elements and typography.

-

Design

Philip Dam Roadley-Battin & Sun Helen Isdahl Kalvenes

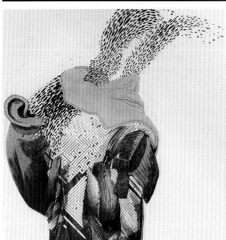

2011

When Saints Go Machine - Kelly Single

Single cover design for the Danish band When Saints Go Machine. Designed using a photocopying machine.

-

Client

When Saints Go Machine, !K7, EMI Music

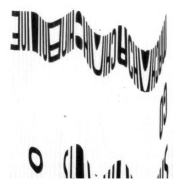

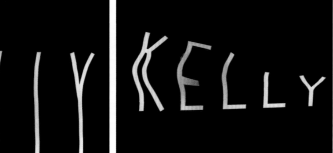

2008

[Above] <u>Typography vs. Human Anatomy</u>

An interpretation of human anatomy and typography. The end result may be far away from the poses, but nevertheless I got to wear women's stockings for a day, and look rather silly.

2011

<u>When Saints Go Machine - Konkylie</u>

Cover art for When Saints Go Machine's second album release "Konkylie". The cover art exudes a creepy beauty through analogue distorted imagery spawned around the production of the album.
-
<u>Client</u>
When Saints Go Machine, !K7, EMI Music
<u>Drawings and Photography</u>
Nicolaj Manuel Vonsild, Thomas Skou

PHILIP BATTIN

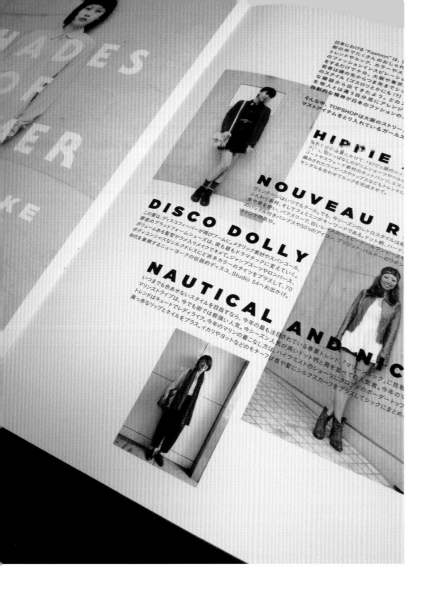

JOHANNA BONNEVIER
Sweden

◇◇◇◇◇◇◇◇◇◇

Johanna Bonnevier is a Swedish art director and graphic designer based in East London. She mainly works with architecture, culture and fashion based projects, ranging from both a small and large scale print jobs to film credits and installations. She was educated at Central Saint Martin's and Camberwell College of Art and Design. Since graduating, she has worked for Black Dog Publishing and Topshop. She is also running her own studio where she has worked with clients such as Fashion East, b Store, Embassy of Sweden, Färgfabriken, 42 Architects and The Bartlett School of Architecture, and UCL amongst others.

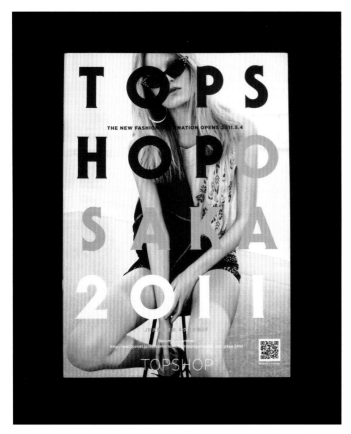

2011

Topshop Osaka

Marketing and PR materials for
Topshop's store opening in Osaka.
–
Client
Topshop

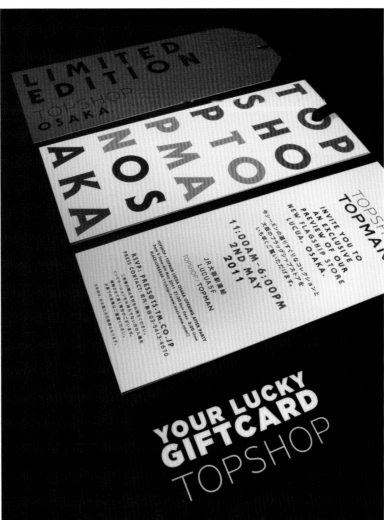

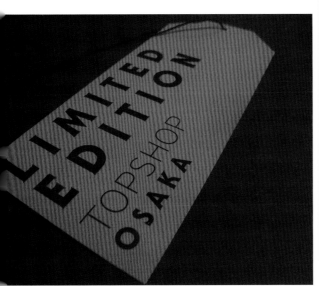

2011

Topshop Sergelgatan

Marketing material for Topshop
store opening in Sergelgatan,
Stockholm, Sweden.
-
<u>Client</u>
Topshop

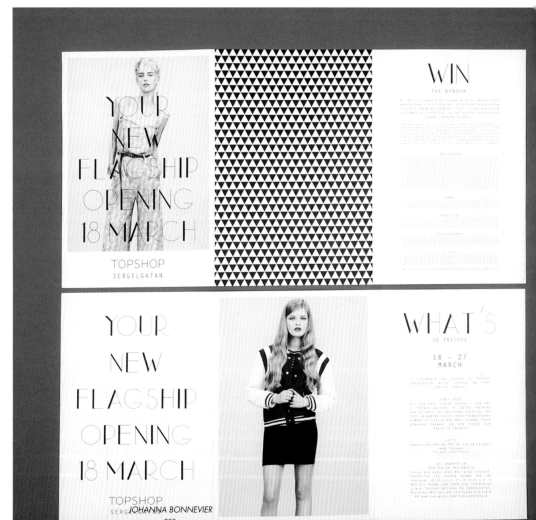

WIN THE WINDOW
HÄMTA DIN TÄVLINGSKUPONG I BUTIKEN

TOPSHOP

FREDAG 18 MARS —— SÖNDAG 27 MARS

STYLA DIN EGEN LOOK I TOPSHOPS GODBITAR OCH POSERA
SEN I VÅRT FOTOBÅS OCH TA MED ETT MINNE HEM FRÅN DIN
UPPLEVELSE I DEN NYA TOPSHOP-BUTIKEN PÅ SERGELGATAN.
KOLLA IN VÅRT GALLERI OCH TAGGA DIG SJÄLV PÅ
WWW.FACEBOOK.COM/TOPSHOPSVERIGE

TOPSHOP

HANDLA FÖR MER ÄN 500KR
OCH FÅ EN GÅVA FRÅN TOPSHOP
*SÅ LÄNGE LAGRET RÄCKER

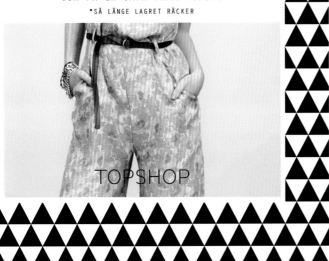

TOPSHOP

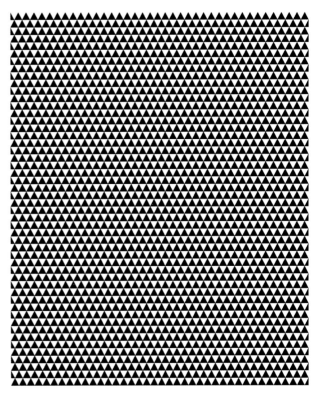

GRATTIS, DU HAR VUNNIT EN SHOPPINGUPPLEVELSE FÖR
5000KR I VÅR NYA TOPSHOP-BUTIK PÅ SERGELGATAN.
VISA UPP DETTA PRESENTKORT I KASSAN.
*INGA KONTANTER KAN GES I VÄXEL
*GILTIGT T.O.M. 31 MARS 2011

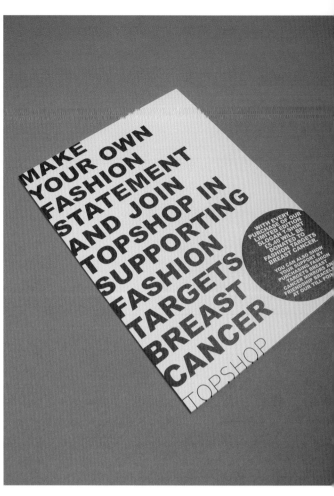

2011

[Opposite page]

**Topshop supports Fashion Targets
Breast Cancer**

Marketing material for Topshop supporting
"Fashion Targets Breast Cancer".
-
Client
Topshop

2010

As the Plot Unfolds

Poster for the launch of 42 Architects
installation in The Local Firm's pop-up shop
in Bruno Gallerian, Stockholm.
-
Client
42 Architects / The Local Firm

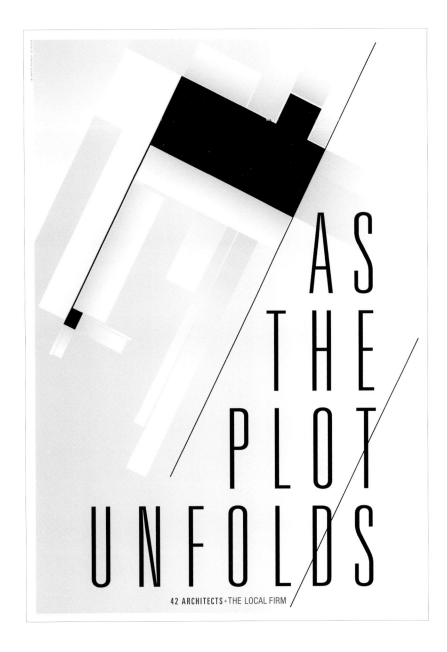

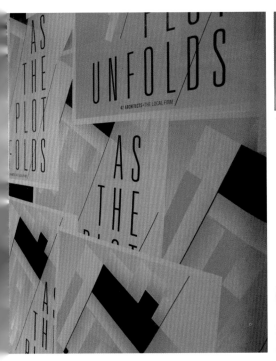

SELECTED WORKS
SPRING / SUMMER 2009

42

42

PRACTICE PROFILE & CONTACT DETAILS

2008–2011
42 Architects
Logo, stationery, website,
press and PR material.
-
Client
42 Architects

CONTACT
42 ARCHITECTS
STUDIO 2, PICKWICK HOUSE
2C EBENEZER STREET
LONDON N1 7MP, UK

SELECTED CLIENTS
A STORE, LONDON, UK

ANOTHER ROOM
HOLOCAUST MEMORIAL
COMPETITION PROPOSAL
ATLANTIC CITY, USA

BOSCOMBE SANDS
ACCESSIBLE BEACH HUT
DESIGN COMPETITION
BOURNEMOUTH, UK

THE BOARDROOM
TEMPORARY PAVILION
CLERKENWELL COMPETITION PROPOSAL
LONDON DESIGN WEEK, UK

ENDLESSNESS
WINDOW INSTALLATION
A STORE
LONDON, UK

DIN SCOOTER
SHOWROOM
STOCKHOLM, SWEDEN

ÖSTBERGET
MASTERPLAN, LANDSCAPE AND BUILDING DESIGN
ÖSTERSUND, SWEDEN

GASHOLDER NO 8
PUBLIC EVENT SPACE
LONG-LISTED COMPETITION PROPOSAL
LONDON, UK

42

VÄSTRA SKATEPARK
LANDSCAPE DESIGN
FALUN, SWEDEN

GREENER THAN THOU
EXHIBITION DESIGN AND CURATION
LONDON, UK AND PARIS, FRANCE

KÄLLVIKEN
HOUSE RE-MODELLING AND EXTENSION
FALUN, SWEDEN

WWW.42ARCHITECTS.COM

Plork

T-shirt prints on the theme of Play/Work.
-
Client
Plork

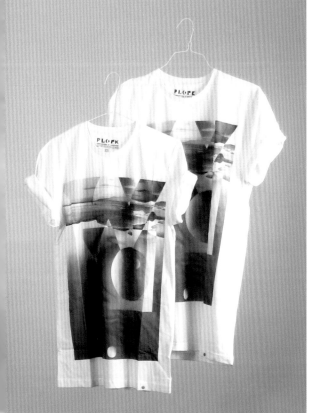

2011

Secret Store

Marketing and PR material for
"Secret Store" in London and New
York.

-

<u>Client</u>
Topshop

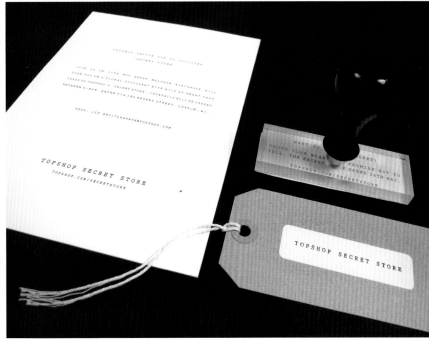

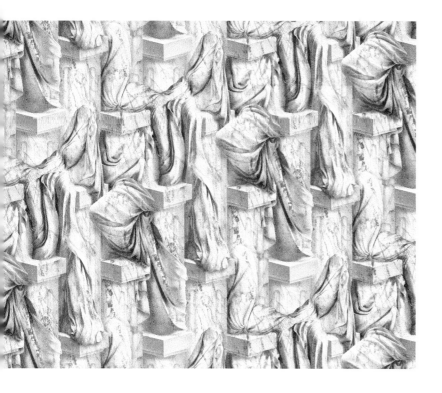

JOHAN HJERPE
Sweden

◇◇◇◇◇◇◇◇◇◇◇◇◇

Johan Hjerpe is a brand concept developer, art director and partner of his own brand and service development agency Imaginary Life. Along with conceptual work, Johan is highly active within the cultural field, driving projects as diverse as designing prints and fabrics for fashion, set design, magazine art direction, graphic design and concept development for various art and fashion projects.

2011

Diana Orving – You a/w 2011

Bodyless marble drapings for Diana Orving a/w 2011 collection "YOU".

-

Client
Diana Orving

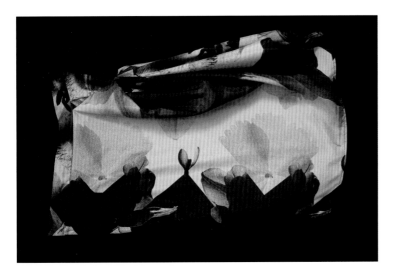

2009

[Left & Above]

<u>Diana Orving – Curtains s/s 2010</u>

Flower pattern in collaboration with
photographer Patricia Reyes for Diana Orving
s/s 2010 collection "Curtains".

-
<u>Client</u>
Diana Orving

2008

[Bottom]

<u>Diana Orving – Spaces s/s 2009</u>

Fashion as spatiality, pleats and corridors for
Diana Orving s/s 2009 collection "Spaces".

-
<u>Client</u>
Diana Orving

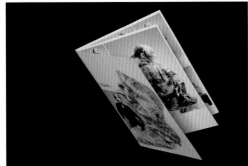

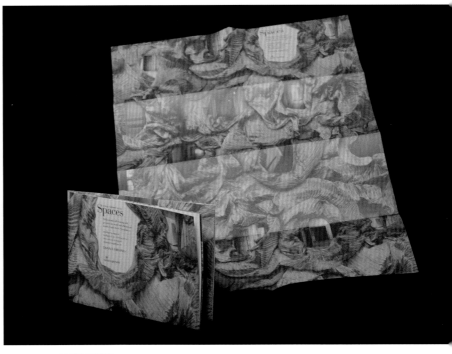

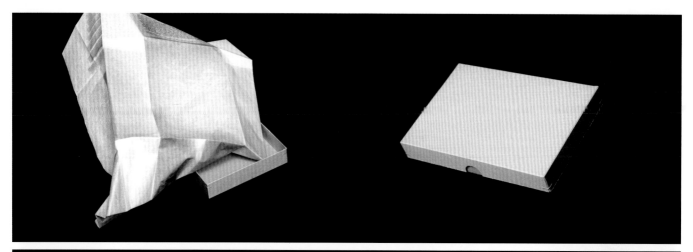

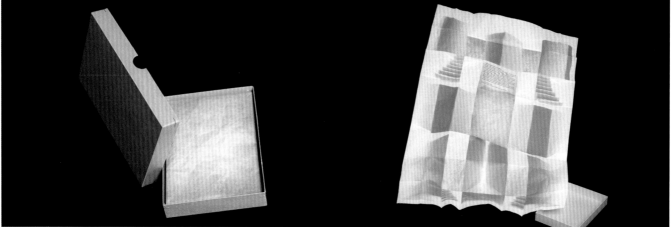

2009

[Above] <u>Boys Don't Cry – Box of Untold</u>
<u>Stories</u>

Silk screened, cut-off stairs and pathways on silk
tracing paper for the theme "untold stories".

-
<u>Client</u>
Architecture firm self-promotion

2007

[Bottom] <u>Snöfrid – Magazine No0</u>

Snöfrid Magazine No0, the performance manual.
Visual concept in collaboration with Ylva Ogland.

-
<u>Client</u>
Snöfrid – Magazine No0

2007

+46 Awards – Nikoline Liv
Andersen Fashion Show

A doll catwalk on top of the catwalk for
2 doll themed collections by Nikoline
Liv Andersen.

-
Client
Nikoline Liv Andersen

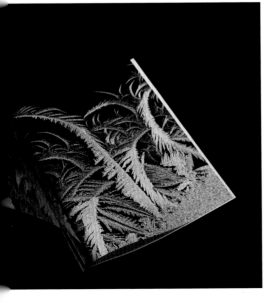

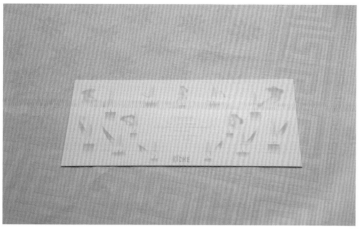

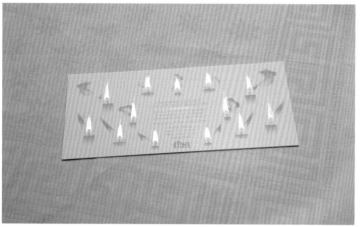

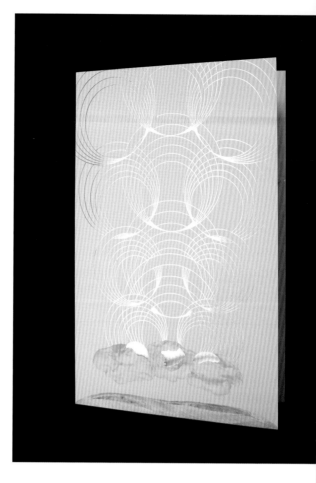

2008

Riche – New Year

New Year's Eve invitation for the restaurant Riche. The foiled candle flames are in different colors: silver for the invitation, white for the dinner ticket, and a rainbow hued mirror for the party ticket.

—
<u>Client</u>
Riche Restaurant

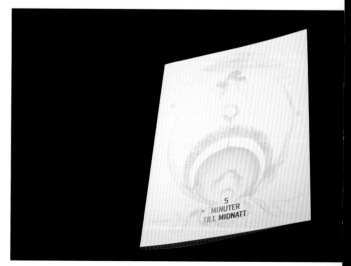

2007

[Above] <u>The Royal University College of Fine Arts, Stockholm - MA Exhibition</u>

Exhibition catalogue and visual concept for MA graduation show "5 Minutes to Midnight".
-
<u>Client</u>
The Royal University College of Fine Arts

[Bottom] <u>Stina Persson Helleday</u>

Business card design for the stylist and set designer Stina Persson Helleday.

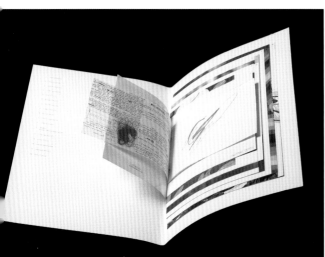

PHONG PHAN
Denmark

〰〰〰〰〰〰〰

Phong Phan is a Danish graphic design student set to graduate in 2013 at the School of Visual Communication in Haderslev, Denmark. Before attending his studies in Haderslev he had a foundation year in graphic design at the Scandinavian Design College in Randers, Denmark. He also runs his own website – www.phongphan.dk – where he operates as a freelance graphic designer.

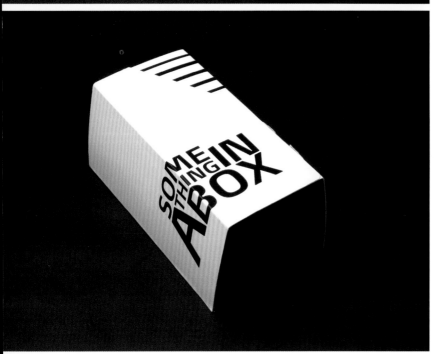

2010
In Your Hands

Visual identity and package design for a creative clothing company. Made as a school project at the Scandinavian Design College.

2010

Scandinavian Design College Anniversary

In 2010 the Scandinavian Design College had its 10th anniversary. To celebrate the anniversary the school produced a series of creative give-aways for their biannual student exhibition, SHOW OFF. Packaging and logo were designed for the anniversary give-aways.

Client
Scandinavian Design College
Design
Mia Bjergegaard, Phong Phan

2010
Damgaard Bøfhus
Logotype and business card design
for a local steak house situated in
Vejle, Denmark.
-
<u>Client</u>
Damgaard Bøfhus

DAM
GAARD

BØFHUS

2011

UD Magazine

UD Magazine is a creative magazine about
live action role play. The intention with
this magazine is to bring inspiration and
interesting articles to its readers within the role
play community. Made as a school project at
the School of Visual Communication.

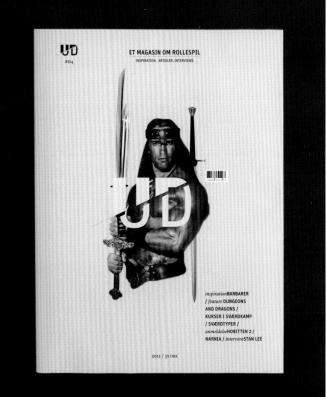

SNASK

Sweden

◇◇◇◇◇◇◇◇◇◇◇◇

SNASK is a brand, design, and film agency situated in the heart of Stockholm. Their work is frequently internationally referenced and results in brand platforms, graphic identities, short films, handmade photo installations, communication strategies, design manuals, stop motions, TV commercials and carefully crafted corporate love-stories. Hello and Snask off!

SNASK

2010

Stockholm Culture Night

In 2010 Stockholm created
Stockholm Culture Night. The city
wanted their night to be playful,
cutting-edge and as inspiring as
the New York and Amsterdam
equivalents.
Snask was asked to conceptualize
the project. During the first breath
of a new born brand two things
are important: repeating the name
and building a clear image to
cut through the haze and make
people aware of the brand. We
did this by creating a graphic
identity, design manual and
communication focusing on one
thing – simplicity. It will continue
in 2011 and Snask's dreams are
purple, fantasizing about next
year's continuing success.

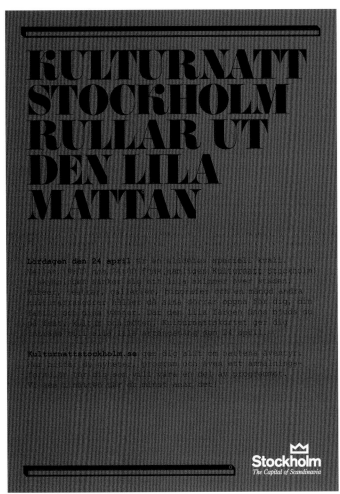

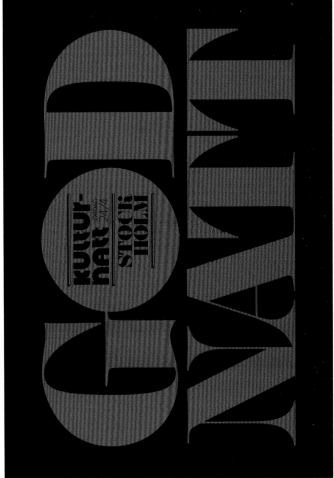

2009

Malmö Festival

Malmö festival is the largest city festival in Scandinavia. With 1.5 million visitors each year it is a hugely popular event during 8 days in August. We worked with them all throughout the year in 2009 as well as in 2010. We remade their identity into being more art and design focused but keeping it public and playful. Everything is made by hand and nothing is 3D or digital, including the pure installations which were photographed.
The assignment included identity, concept, tone of voice, graphic design, magazine, ads, films, and environmental design.
-
Client
City of Malmö
Creative Director
Fredrik Öst, Magnus Berg
Design
Jens Nilsson
Photography
Axel Engström
Account Manager
Erik Kockum

2010

Malmö Festival

Malmö festival is the largest city festival in Scandinavia. With 1.5 million visitors each year it is a hugely popular event during 8 days in August. We worked with them all throughout the year in 2009 as well as in 2010. We remade their identity into being more art and design focused but keeping it public and playful. Everything is made by hand and nothing is 3D or digital, including the pure installations which were photographed.

The assignment included identity, concept, tone of voice, graphic design, magazine, ads, films, and environmental design.

-

<u>Client</u>
City of Malmö
<u>Creative Director</u>
Fredrik Ost, Magnus Berg
<u>Design</u>
Jens Nilsson
<u>Photography</u>
Axel Engström
<u>Account Manager</u>
Erik Kockum

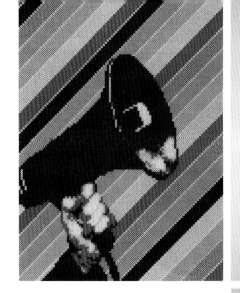

2009

Bruno Götgatsbacken

The ultra hip shopping center Bruno
Götgatsbacken was looking for a new brand
and design agency to produce print campaigns
and indoor events.
We conceptualized Bruno Götgatsbacken
into a man called Bruno that loved pearling,
drinking red wine and horseback riding.
Everything Bruno said was said through
pearling, and his lovely horse was hardly ever
in the stable, because she was used as a visual
A-frame. She got re-painted once a month by
several famous artists, and has become iconic
and a symbol for the shopping center.

—
Client
Bruno Götgatsbacken

2009

Liberal Youth Party

In 2008 the Liberal Youth Party realized that their graphic identity and communication was dated and didn't appeal to modern youths. They needed change badly and they asked Snask to be their change agent. When conceptualizing the Liberal Youth Party we quickly realized that the word politics could be intimidating. We de-dramatized the word politics and made both the Liberal Youth Party and politics sexy and interesting. Since the start of our relationship the Liberal Youth Party has increased their number of total members by close to 200%, explained by both an increased retainment rate and increased attraction of new members.

Client
Liberal Youth Party

2009

Luger / Live Nation

Every year Luger hosts a party where they announce next year's acts and upcoming bands. We were asked to help them attract promoters and booking agents to attend the party. Snask started by asking what the no.1 problem that promoters and booking agents face. The research led us to the insight that promoters suffer from anxiety – not knowing what will sell or fill the arena in the next year. To relieve their anxiety we packaged next year's artists as a medicine called Bandil 250db. The invitation was sent out in a 1977 looking medicine box on Ecstasy.

–
<u>Client</u>
Luger

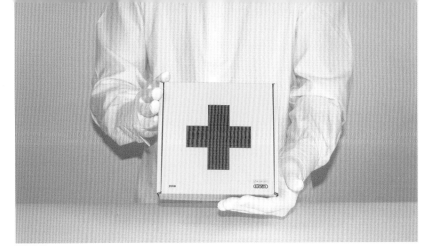

YOUR FRIENDS
Norway

~~~

YOUR FRIENDS is an Oslo, Norway based graphic design studio, founded by Carl Gürgens and Henrik Fjeldberg. The studio works in different fields of graphic design and develops solutions for identities, exhibitions, book design, editorial design, posters, music packaging, websites, typefaces etc. Their work is focused around cultural and commercial projects, as well as self-initiated projects, specializing in print.

They believe in strong ideas and strive to push boundaries within solutions based on conceptual thinking. The studio works with both national and international clients, and the design projects of YOUR FRIENDS have been published and exhibited in Germany, France, UK, Japan, China, USA etc.

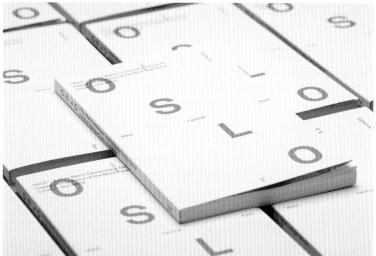

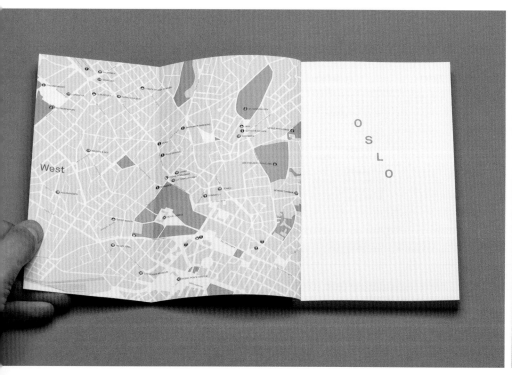

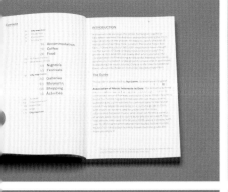

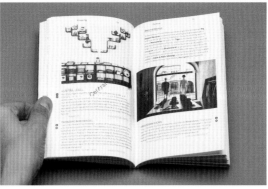

2009

Oslo - A Poor Mans Connoisseur Guide

After the success of our Oslo Guide from 2009 we were asked to update the guide and release a 2nd edition in conduction with Øya Festivalen 2010. In collaboration with Music Oslo and Sondre Sommerfelt (the editor), we updated the design and content to make it more functional and make room for bigger photos. The basis of the idea is to capture the diffenreces between west and east part in the city, which goes way back in history regarding cultural and social aspects. One of those factors, which in itself has been a important part of the city, is Akerselva, the river which splits the city in two. Format: 105×180 mm, 96 pages.

-

Client
ByLarm Music Oslo
Editor
Sondre Sommerfelt
Photography
Einar Aslaksen

2010
Salone Satellite, Milano 2010 - Petter Skogstad

Petter Skogstad is a young and promising product designer. We designed his identity for his launch at Salone Satellite Milano 2010. His work questions the role of furniture, and how subtle design can be. A design's strength lies, not only in how much an object is designed, but also how ordinary design can be when being used in everyday life. These thoughts follow the traditions and ideology of Supernormal. We designed posters, business cards and compliment slips for the Milano exhibition as well as giving advice on the stand in order to make everything come together as a strong identity. The stand was nominated best in show by Monocle.
In collaboration with StokkeAustad.

-
Client
Petter Skogstad
Photography
Einar Aslaksen

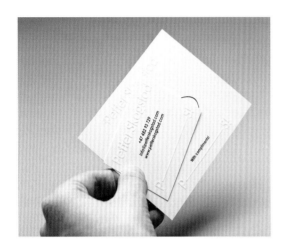

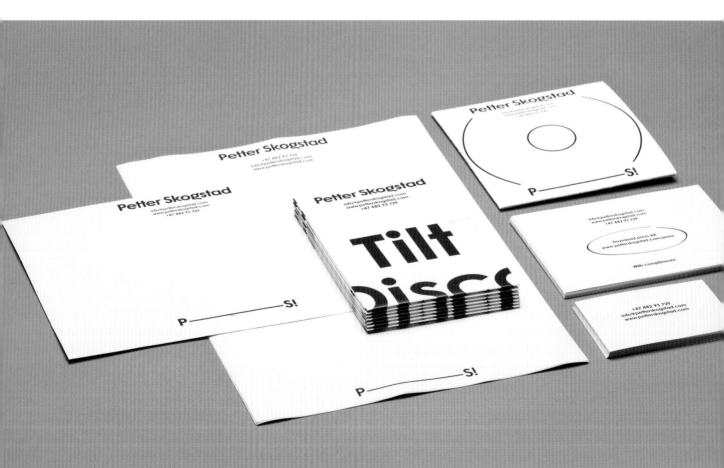

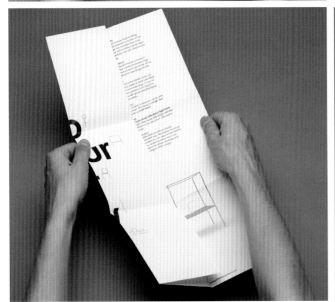

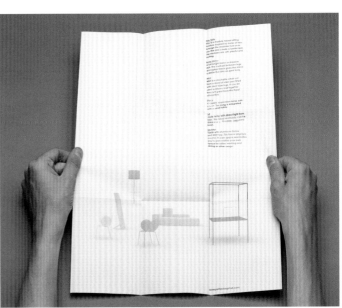

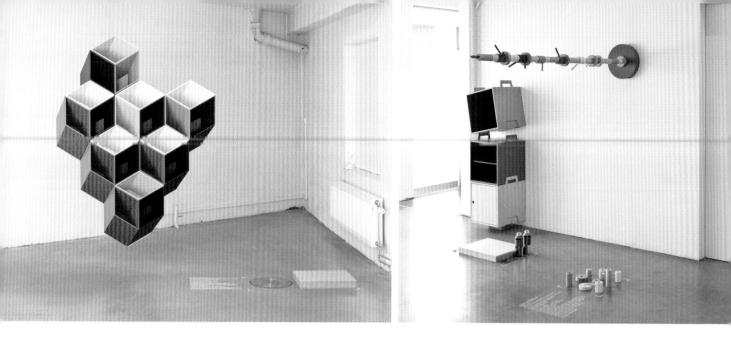

2010

ODL-Utformasjon

We were asked to curate and design an exhibition in collaboration with product designers StokkeAustad and ODL at Galleri ROM (Rom for Kunst og arkitektur). The line-up of designers who exhibited consisted of both up and coming designers and veterans in the Norwegian design scene. The title refers to information and design, which is the core of the exhibition. The exhibition questions how we see things, and how our perception can be challenged with small variations from what we define as "ordinary". The end result was an exhibition showing products in an unusual way to give the viewer a new perspective on the products, and tell a new and in depth story.

-
Client
Oslo Designerlaug and ROM Gallery for Architecture
Photography
Henrik Fjeldberg

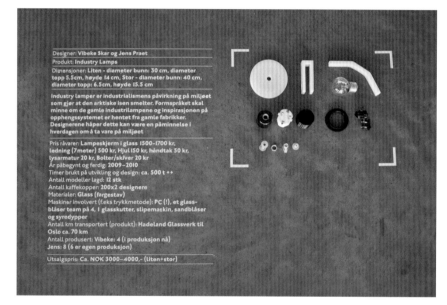

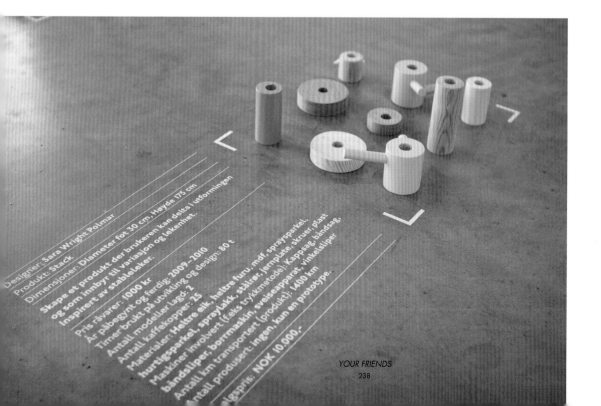

YOUR FRIENDS
238

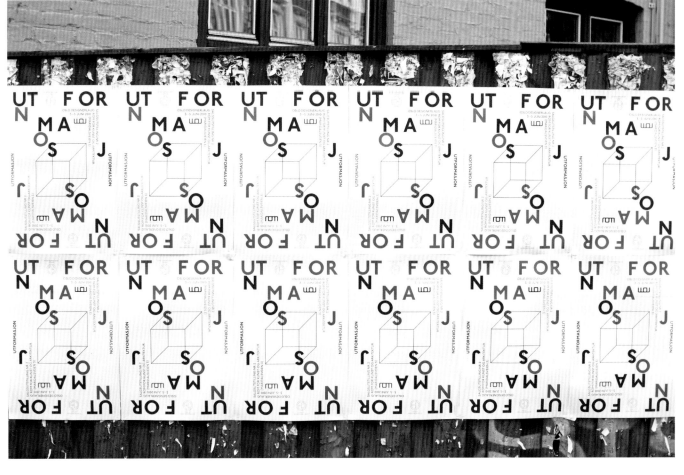

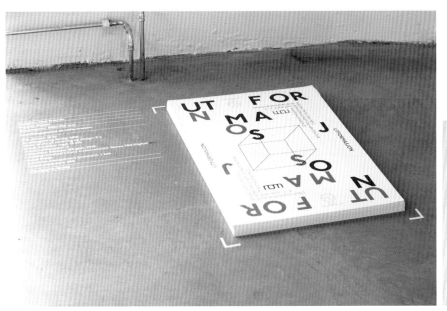

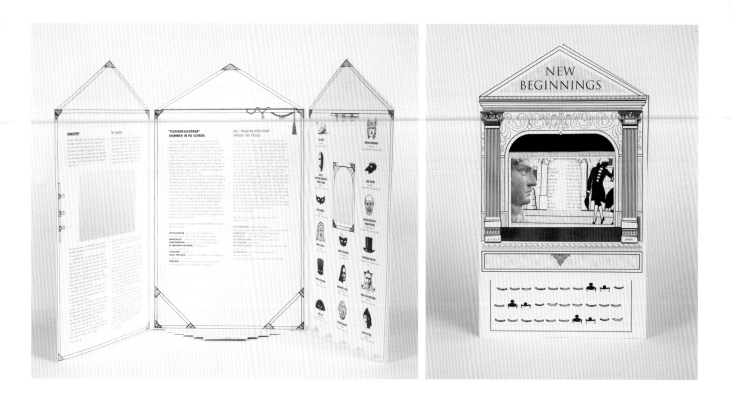

BYGGSTUDIO

Sweden

◇◇◇◇◇◇◇◇◇◇◇◇◇

Byggstudio is a design studio that works with two and three
dimensional graphic design and concept design.
Byggstudio´s design is characterized by a curious and playful
attitude, emphasizing personal and parallel stories. Their own
research for each project is significant to the result in form and
function where communicating a central idea is the starting
point rather than the medium.
Byggstudio was founded by graphic designers Hanna Nilsson
and Sofia Østerhus in 2006. They both hold an MFA in visual
communication from Danmarks Designskole in 2006.

2010

[Top left of the opposite page]

Iaspis Open House 2010

Program folder for Iaspis Open House 2010. Created as a paper theater, the curatorial theme of the exhibition was the exhibit as a stage and the artists as actors. The folder holds a manuscript.

The folder is made like a paper theatre where the stamped pages form the stage. The inside of the folder represents the back-stage with props and the actors/ artists portrayed as classical theatre masks. The folder holds a manuscript.

-
Client
Iaspis
Photography
Lotten Pålsson

2010

The Story of a Mug kafé

To launch and market the release of The Story of a Mug, Byggstudio and Apartamento hosted a pop-up café during 3 days in December 2010. The café concept is a live interpretation of the themes and articles in the book, foremost the chapter focusing on the historic development of the Mug. The café, therefore, creates a time-travel experience through the history of design and coffee-culture.

The table works as a schematic timeline, from 1700-2010. The guests were welcome to sit down and experience different style periods, coffee and cakes.

-
Client
Iittala
Photography
Lotten Pålsson

2008-2011

Malmö Folkets Park - Graphic Identity

The People's Park is a fun and open place for everyone and that should
show! We wanted to create a warm, welcoming and fun graphic
identity for the park, using references to classic people's park (Folkpark)
aesthetics in Sweden.
The park needed a lively voice to greet its visitors and communicate
news and seasonal activities. We made a flexible signage system for the
entrance, functioning as a public
notice board. It utilizes 3 flexible program boards with screenprinted
letters and a variety of signs fixed to the wooden grid.

Client
Malmö Folkets Park

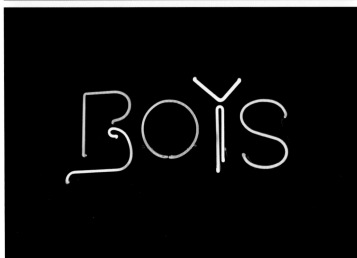

HJÄRTA SMÄRTA
Sweden

◇◇◇◇◇◇◇◇◇◇◇◇◇

Hjärta Smärta is an award winning independent graphic design studio in Stockholm, Sweden, established in 2001 by Angela Tillman Sperandio and Samira Bouabana. Hjärta Smärta has extensive experience working with a wide range of commissions, from company profiles to exhibition graphics and book design.
Hjärta Smärta applies a high level of commitment to each assignment. They are often commissioned by clients to take part in the projects from the early conceptual stage. They believe in strong ideas executed with a traditional approach. Their solutions are often classic in design but with a playful twist.

2008
[Left] Neon Letters
A letter system made out of recycled neon signs.
Ongoing project.

2010
[Bottom] Kolla!
Graphic identity for an annual Swedish competition for graphic design, illustration and animation.
In collaboration with Lisa Rydell.

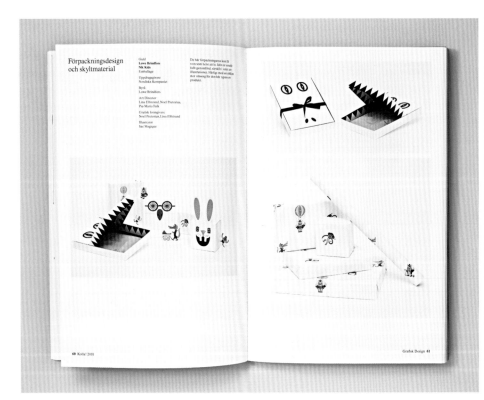

2011

Arkitekturmuseet live

Identity and exhibition graphics for Arkitekturmuseet Live (The Swedish Museum of Architecture) in Stockholm. The exhibition was a new type of exhibition where the museum worked as a platform for discussions, lectures, film shows and workshops that were streamed for audiences online. Seven weeks were devoted to diverse themes, such as Sustainable Fashion or Urban Development.

2010

History of Sweden

Identity and exhibition graphics for a new
exhibition featuring the history of Sweden from
1000-2010 AD that recently opened at the
Museum of National Antiquities. We were
asked to create the graphic identity as well as
the exhibition graphics with Mikael Varhelyi,
who did the Exhibition design.
-
Exhibition Design
Mikael Varhelyi

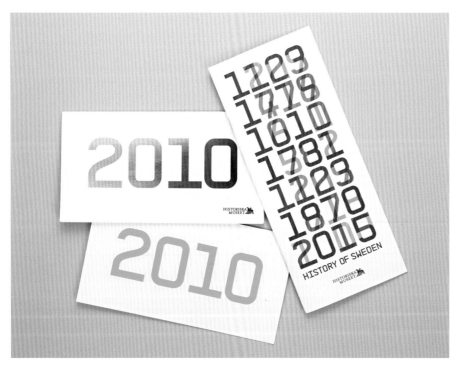

2010
The Flight Lab

Identity and exhibition graphics for The Flight Lab (Flyglabbet), a section of the Swedish Air Force Museum in Linköping. The bold and colorful typography is inspired by aircraft graphics from planes exhibited in other part of the museum and by the notion of motion.

Exhibition Design
Daniel Djupdal

Luftträff
Air impact

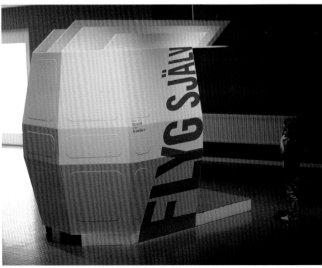

INDEX

Haltenbanken
Bergen, Norway

www.haltenbanken.com

Hjärta Smärta
Stockholm, Sweden

www.hjartasmarta.se

Johan Hjerpe
Stockholm, Sweden

www.johanhjerpe.com

Henrik Nygren Design
Stockholm, Sweden

henriknygren.se

Hvass&Hannibal
Copenhagen, Denmark

www.hvasshannibal.dk

Johanna Bonnevier
London, UK / Sweden

www.johannabonnevier.com

Heydays
Oslo, Norway

www.heydays.info

Janine Rewell
Helsinki, Finland

www.janinerewell.com

Johannes Ekholm
Helsinki, Finland

www.tsto.org

Oh Yeah Studio
Oslo, Norway

www.ohyeahstudio.no

Phong Phan
Haderslev, Denmark

www.phongphan.dk

Siggi Odds
Reykjavík, Iceland

www.siggiodds.com

Oscar Pastarus
Stockholm, Sweden

oscarpastarus.com

Re-public
Copenhagen, Denmark

www.re-public.com

Simon Renström
Berlin, Germany / Stockholm, Sweden

www.simonrenstrom.se

Philip Battin
Copenhagen, Denmark

battin.dk

Research and Development
Stockholm, Sweden

www.researchanddevelopment.se

Snasen
Oslo, Norway

snasen.no

SNASK
Stockholm, Sweden

www.snask.com
P. 226-233

Tuukka Koivisto
Helsinki, Finland

www.tuukkakoivisto.com
P. 62-65

Your Friends
Oslo, Norway

www.yourfriends.no
P. 234-239

The Emperor of Antarctica
Copenhagen, Denmark

emperorofantarctica.com
P. 172-175

Viggo Mörck
London, UK / Sweden

www.viggomorck.com
P.136-139

Tsto
Helsinki, Finland

www.tsto.org
P. 36-45

WE RECOMMEND
Copenhagen, Denmark

www.werecommend.se
P. 20-201

ACKNOWLEDGEMENTS

We would like to acknowledge our gratitude to the artists and designers for their generous contributions of images, ideas and concepts. We are very grateful to many other people whose names do not appear on the credits but who provided assistance and support. Thanks also go to people who have worked hard on the book and put ungrudging efforts into it. Without you all, the creation and ongoing development of this book would not have been possible and thank you for sharing your innovation and creativity with all our readers.

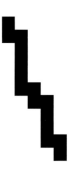